Ron,
Thank you for
accounting me to tell
the story in this book.
I appreciate our
friendship.

Unselling

THE INDEPENDENT CONSULTANT'S
GUIDE TO TRUSTING GOD FOR MORE
BUSINESS, FAITH, AND LIFE

JOHN D. HUGHES

ILLUSTRATIONS BY YSABEL MORALES

Unselling: The independent consultant's guide to trusting God for more business, faith, and life / John D. Hughes; illustrations by Ysabel Morales.

All scripture passages are taken from The Holy Bible, New International Version®, NIV® Copyright ©1973, 1978, 1984, 2011 by *Biblica, Inc.*®

The strategies within this publication may not be suitable in all cases. Always consult with an appropriate professional for your specific situation.

Some anecdotes in this book are true to life and included with the permission of the individuals involved. All other anecdotes are amalgamations of true situations and any resemblance to individuals living or dead is purely coincidental.

ISBN: 978-1-7322426-0-9
ISBN: 978-1-7322426-1-6 (ebook)

Library of Congress Control Number: 2018908850

Printed in the United States of America

First Edition

10 9 8 7 6 5 4 3 2 1

Cover Design & Formatting By Damonza.com

*For my God
and His Son, Jesus Christ,
and Their gift of grace,
by which I'm saved.*

CONTENTS

PREFACE

FEAR IS A killer. It takes countless lives every day. I watched what it did to my dad.

My dad was a printer by trade. Starting as a teenager in southeast Iowa, through some fifty years and into his final days in western Ohio, he set the tiny metal characters into place, loaded the paper, and ran the print jobs—newspapers, business cards, advertisements, ballots during voting season, you name it.

He never made more than $15 an hour, even in 2001 when he retired. He worked sixty-hour weeks. Week after week. Year after year. Decade after decade.

We lived at the bottom of middle class, on the cusp of poor. I never once heard my dad complain about money though. I don't ever remember going hungry. Or experiencing a birthday or Christmas without gifts. We never had money to spare; we had the basics covered, nothing more.

In the summer of 1974 I turned twelve. My dad and his friend, Ron, a fellow printer, started helping at a local commercial print shop. The owner was aging and needed their part-time help to keep the business going. My dad invited me to help out a few times. He showed me all that he did to prepare the paper and machines for each run.

I soaked up this time with my dad. I loved the work and loved learning from him, and just being in his domain.

A few weeks into this adventure, Ron and my dad sat in our kitchen talking. The owner had asked them if they'd like to buy his business. I don't remember any of the conversations they had. I *do* remember the vision I created in my mind of working with my dad every day at the shop. Rather than a short-term effort on his part, this would be a family business. And just like my dad, I would come home every evening, steeped in the aroma of paper and oil.

Then nothing.

Talk about buying the business stopped.

Talk about the shop stopped.

No more planning. No more visits from Ron.

His work at the shop stopped too.

My dad went back to his sixty-hour-a-week job. And that's how life went. That's how a life ended. At least, it felt like a death to me. I know my dad chose his family and the safety of a job over risk and the uncertainties of buying and running a business—something he'd never been exposed to. It just wasn't him. He was a blue-collar guy, born and bred. His own father managed no more than a career of odd jobs.

My vision of working next to my dad in a busy print shop—*his print shop*—died.

He was already carrying the weight and worry of household bills—that fifty-pound bag of rocks on his shoulders—every day, all day. And then sleeping with it on his chest all night. It never left him. Carrying the additional weight of his own business would mean lugging around another fifty-pound bag.

I never again experienced that time with my dad, never again stepped into his domain, never learned anything more about business from him. He went back to his safe, quiet life.

I wish he'd jumped. I wish he could have found a way to look past the fear. I wish he'd taken the risk to learn all that he needed to know to be successful, even if it meant failure. I wish he would

have jumped and found faith, faith in the God he didn't know…
and faith in himself.

Fear is a killer. That emotional warrior can rise up at just the right time and save us from true danger; but all too often it fails us, it oversteps its bounds and stops us from pursuing our dreams, dreams that bring life, abundant life.

I took the leap that my dad didn't take. I wanted this abundant life that our God offers us. But I wonder even today if I did this for my dad. If I was doing this as a sort of redemption for him. Maybe I did what I so desperately had wanted him to do for himself back in that summer of 1974.

I stepped out on my own as an independent consultant in January 2005, after twenty-three years in corporate America. For the first three years of my business I wanted out; I wanted to quit. I wanted off the ride. And nearly every day I did quit: I emotionally gave up.

It was a difficult and hard ride.

Somewhere in year four though, I realized that as badly as I wanted off, I was still on the ride. It's an odd feeling to want to give up on something yet find yourself still holding on.

I realized that something else was happening.

I was expecting a business journey, an entrepreneurial journey. But God had different plans. Bigger plans. Better plans. He was taking me on a faith journey.

Our faith isn't proven or even challenged until there's nothing left to lean on *except* that faith. For me, that faith is in the God of the Bible, in His Son, and in Their promises for us, beautifully woven together in a seamless story.

Every indie consultant or small business owner I know starts out with grand visions of how their business will unfold, only to be hit almost immediately with a season or more of struggle, frustration, and doubt. Serious doubt about this path we've chosen.

However, it's what we do with the doubt that determines whether we'll survive or not. We can allow the doubt to consume us until it drives us to our knees in fear and then to the surrender of our dreams. Or, we can overcome the doubt with faith and trust in Him and His promises.

The thief comes only to steal and kill and destroy; I have
come that they may have life, and have it to the full.

John 10:10

That promise from Jesus became key not only to my business but my life. I leaned on it. I trusted it. I pursued it. And in pursuing this full, abundant life that He desperately desires for us, I found myself pursuing Him more as well.

I had been a Christian for twenty-four years when I launched my indie consulting business. But it wasn't until I chose to truly trust Him and His promises in year four that my journey to this abundant life began, as did the unselling life that He unfolded before me.

As I pursued Him and this freedom He generously offers us, God also pursued me. I know, because I experienced it.

Of the multitude of times I quit in my mind, three times I actually took the action to find a full-time job. I was simply out of money. All three times, the same friend called with consulting work. It was that third time in 2008 that I finally said, "OK, God. I get it. I'm supposed to be doing this. You want me here. I believe you. I *trust* you."

From that moment forward, and it's now been ten years, I never doubted Him or this path I was on. I trusted that no matter what happened, He would take care of my family and me.

He had used my deep desire for a business to draw me closer to Himself and to grow me spiritually.

There was a beauty in this journey that still amazes me. I am in awe of what He did and how He did it. He truly is an awesome God when we simply get out of the way and allow Him to be just that.

He led me from simply believing *in* Him to flat out *believing* Him.

Faith is without a doubt key to this unselling life—believing Him and His promises, that He means them for our good, to bring about the abundant life that He offers us.

> *Which of you, if your son asks for bread, will give him*
> *a stone? Or if he asks for a fish, will give him a snake?*
> *If you, then, though you are evil, know how to give*
> *good gifts to your children, how much more will your*
> *Father in heaven give good gifts to those who ask him!*
>
> Matthew 7:9-11

For me, this idea of unselling is about so much more than business and certainly more than "not selling." It's about fullness of life. However, this full, abundant life that God promises those who have accepted Jesus Christ as Savior doesn't come by our own brute force. It can't. It won't. I tried. And failed. It comes about by letting go and trusting, by believing that which He created us to be and to do will come alive in us when we fully surrender our lives to Him, trust Him, and trust His promises.

> *Trust in the Lord with all your heart and lean not*
> *on your own understanding; in all your ways submit*
> *to him, and he will make your paths straight.*
>
> Proverbs 3:5-6

John
August 10, 2018

HOW TO USE THIS BOOK

Unselling was designed to be read front-to-back, but it doesn't need to be. You can scan the Table of Contents and jump directly to chapters that most interest you. Either way, sequentially or randomly, you will ultimately learn the specifics of the "indie engine" that will usher you into the "unselling" life.

At the end of each chapter, you'll find questions for guidance and action, as well as a couple of blank pages for note taking. Use these questions to guide your steps and to create your own action/business plan.

Finally, the Appendix lists a few of the books that have been important to me throughout my career, business, and faith journey. You may find some of them helpful and encouraging for yourself as well.

I do suggest that you read through the book once, review the chapter questions, and take initial notes. Along the way, highlight the chapters and questions/actions you'd like to prioritize. (Don't try to eat this elephant in one bite! Break it down into manageable, chewable chunks.) Then, return to the chapters and questions/actions that you feel are the next right steps for *you*. Take those prioritized actions, and as you succeed and fail forward, identify and take on your next priorities, building on your successes and lessons learned. And never stop. Never stop taking action, moving forward, making mistakes, learning, growing. Never.

Once you've read through the book and started your action plan, you'll want to keep *Unselling* handy as a reference and source of encouragement.

May God richly bless you on your own faith and business journey!

"Oh, no! Not down on my luck. Just enjoying the freedom of being an independent consultant."

Into the Cold

"For I know the plans I have for you," declares the LORD,
"plans to prosper you and not to harm you,
plans to give you hope and a future."

Jeremiah 29:11

~ Key Point ~

Your faith and trust in God can overcome your fears; your actions in the direction of your dreams prove out that faith and trust.

Leaps of faith

FEW THINGS REPRESENT as giant a leap of faith as willingly and deliberately stopping income.

Cold.

Without knowing where the next paycheck will come from. Or when. Or if.

I did that.

It was January 2005. The comfortable corporate job I held in

Seattle made its way to Orlando. I didn't. I chose to stay among the mountains of the Pacific Northwest. I also didn't want another j-o-b. I decided to strike out on my own as an independent consultant. It was something I had been thinking about for five years. But excuses always stopped me; they held me back.

They're not excuses though. They're really lies. All of them.

"You're not good enough," the first lie tells us. "You don't know how to start a business," says the next one. "You'll embarrass yourself." Then, they pile on. "You'll lose all of your savings. You'll lose your house. You'll lose your family. You'll end up on the street. You'll be a failure. You'll never recover, and your family and friends will watch it all happen."

So, we listen to the lies. We give in to them. We agree with them and head straight back to the life we were just trying to escape.

We give in to the dream destroyers that convince us that we can't do something, so we shouldn't even try.

And we don't.

We continue to dream though. But that's all we do: Dream. We never take action on them, never put feet or hands to them. Which means we never get to live the dream.

Instead, we live the regrets.

In reality, we destroy our own dreams. No one does it for us.

It's a choice we make.

We're the ones believing the lies instead of believing our God, the author of *the* book of truth, filled with promises of freedom and abundant life.

Those of us who belong to Him, however, are called to live by faith and not by fear.

We all get to decide for ourselves. Are we choosing to hold tight to the lies or turning instead to His promises? Are we choosing to buy into the fear or bust out in full faith?

In 2005, in the midst of trying to decide whether to launch my own independent consulting business or get another job, I realized that I had bought into these lies. Hook. Line. And sinker. I failed by not even trying.

I don't like failing, and I desperately didn't want to be out begging for a job. So, I jumped.

I was happy in those first few days. Excited about this new venture, about the prospects of being on my own. That feeling didn't last long though. Fear struck. Hard. I realized that to be successful I would need clients and *that* would require selling.

I wasn't a salesperson, nor did I want to be one.

I began to worry about whether I would be able to survive on my own. I knew how to *do* the consulting work, but how would I get the business?

I didn't want to sell. And I also didn't want to go back either... back to another corporate job where politics, power plays, and pointless meetings all too often won out over progress. I didn't want to wake up every day and sit in the same office. Stare at the same screen. The same fake laminated pine desk. The same gray stapler. Something felt wrong about that.

There I was. Out in the cold of independent consulting. The security of a full-time job behind me. No income in sight ahead of me.

"This must be how people go from high-paying corporate jobs to living on the street," I often thought to myself.

Total failure felt that real and that close.

I wrestled with fear and sleepless nights for the next three years.

Now, over ten years later, I'm still out in the cold. It's a comfortable cold, though. I enjoy every moment of this life. And I know what freedom feels like. I get to live it every day. I can work from home, in a coffee shop, in another state, in another country, or not at all. And I trust that business will show up. And it does. Without selling.

This was certainly an entrepreneurial journey, but it proved to be more a faith journey. I traveled from deep fear and worry, to trickles of income and glimmers of hope, to freedom and a stronger faith.

The purpose of this book isn't to share all that happened along the way. It's really meant to answer just one question, a question I've been asked countless times over the last several years and continue to be asked:

"How do you get business?!"

I can't answer this question honestly without acknowledging the God who led me, taught me, and gave me reason for greater faith throughout this journey. That's why this is more a book of faith than a business book.

My faith and the answer to how I get business are forever intertwined.

"How do you get business?!"

While I'd been asked that question dozens of times, it wasn't until early 2014 (in my tenth year as an independent consultant) that I knew it was an important question, and one I needed to answer. On the same afternoon, three different people, in three separate conversations sitting in the same coffee shop in downtown Seattle, asked me that exact question.

While they were asking how I get business, I heard a deeper question. "John, how do you, an introverted technology consultant, sell yourself to these corporate clients? You make it seem easy. How do you do it?"

The truth is, I *am* highly introverted and I'm definitely shy in new situations. When I started my own business, I wondered how I could possibly survive on my own. I knew I would need to develop business and market myself. I would need to sit across from executives and pitch them. I would need to sell!

Anxiety and fear still rocket through me today at the prospect of becoming a salesperson. I desperately wanted my own business, but I didn't want to sell.

I just wanted to be myself.

The silver switch

Those who asked me this question didn't want to hear about the years of trial and error or about my setbacks or mistakes. All they wanted was a silver bullet—one shot, one easy solution they could implement and the money would start rolling in.

Instead of a silver bullet that rips through obstacles, I saw this more like a silver switch that you flip on.

They wanted to know how they could replicate what I have. *Now.* Without the years of hard work, mistakes, failures, embarrassing moments, and empty bank accounts. They wanted to know where the switch was located. John must have found it.

Who wouldn't want to flip the switch that opens the floodgates of business? You know: hang the shingle, flip the switch, cash the checks.

We all want a way of skipping the perilous and fearful step of risk, uncertainty, and hard work that launching a new business brings and get right down to generating income. As if those of us who have been out in the cold of independent consulting at some point cross a magic threshold and are ourselves bequeathed with this hidden knowledge.

Yes! I can tell you that there is a switch. And I know where it is.

The heart of the matter

After years of sleepless nights and hard work, I found it. I found it just as easily as Frodo Baggins (J. R. R. Tolkien's hobbit protagonist in *The Lord of the Rings* series) and his eight fellow companions solved the riddle that eventually opened the Doors of Durin, allowing them to enter the tunnels of Moria and continue on their quest to save Middle-earth, the fictional world Tolkien created for his epic novel series.

The riddle before them, written on the ancient stone door in elvish language, was "Speak, friend, and enter."

The group tried for hours in vain to solve the riddle that would open the doors. And the pressure was on... a sea creature lurked at their feet and enemies were attacking and waiting from every angle. The only way forward was through those doors.

Gandalf the Grey eventually solved the riddle by simply saying "Mellon," the elvish word for friend. He spoke the word "friend" in order to enter in. A simple solution, and right there in front of them the whole time!

Yes, Frodo and his companions were right. It's that easy to open doors and overcome obstacles that stand in the way of achieving our goals.

"Where is this similar switch that opens the floodgates of business?" you ask.

It's in your heart and it's deep inside your soul.

It's your desire for your life. Not for your business, mind you. And definitely not for income. No one's last words were ever "I wish I'd spent more time on my business," or "I wish I'd made more money last year," or "I wish I had the time to take on one more client engagement."

Some call it a dream. I call it desire, a more accurate and powerful description of what you *truly* want for your life.

That's right. Not just what you want for your business or career, but for your *life*.

Just as Frodo experienced in his journey out of the Shire (his "hometown" within Middle-earth) to rid their world of "the one ring," there's a purpose deep inside each of us. No matter how shy, introverted, or small we are or think we are, that purpose exists. Most people keep their purpose buried deep inside, not wanting to put in the hard work to bring it about. Or they're embarrassed by it, or frozen in fear. Or they believe the lies, opting instead to listen to the doubting, negative, shaming voices from others, from their past, echoing inside their head. Or maybe they've convinced themselves that the purpose is meant for someone else.

It's not meant for someone else. That purpose—that dream, desire, vision, or craving—is meant for *you!* It is waiting for you to take action, to apply faith and works in the direction of your desire.

The purposes of a person's heart are deep waters,
but one who has insight draws them out.

Proverbs 20:5

I learned through my indie business journey that simply pursuing my desire brought me life. Abundant, fulfilling, healing life. It will do the same for you.

The only thing your dreams are waiting for is action.

As the body without the spirit is dead,
so faith without deeds is dead.

James 2:26

Once you start taking action something unexpected happens. The abundant life begins to unfold before you. It doesn't wait for the dream to come true. This life begins at inception, when you take that first true step in the direction of your desire. And it continues to show up every single day you take another step in that direction.

When you pursue a dream, a desire, especially one kept buried deep inside for years, joy follows. Then life. Then freedom.

Pursuing God's desire for our lives sets us free by giving us a purpose beyond ourselves, bigger than ourselves. It makes us whole. It heals us.

It's a learned process, though, where you learn to trust a little more each day. You can't get ahead of yourself or ahead of God. Step into His promises and joy, life, and freedom will follow.

And I don't mean pursue a desire like you're going to the mall to buy a new pair of shoes. I mean pursue it in the fashion of Frodo's journey to pitch that problematic gold ring into the fires of Mount Doom to save the whole of Middle-earth. It starts out like a meandering stroll out of the Shire, very innocently. No visions of wraiths, wargs, or orcs cross your mind. (These are just some of the nasty creatures that continually pursue and attack Frodo and his gang of do-gooders throughout their journey, doing all they can to kill their hopes and crush their dreams and mission.) They do show up, though. They were out to stop Frodo, and they're out to stop you. The question becomes, how bad do you want it? And just what is it that you want?

You need to be resolutely clear about what you want. Truly honest with yourself. And you need to be willing to fight every wraith, warg, and orc that cross your path in order to achieve it.

For me, having the business wasn't the ultimate desire or dream. It was bigger than that. I wanted something more. Something I knew I'd be willing to fight for.

Why take this journey?

I didn't strike out on my own to pursue money or accolades or to make a name for myself. I could have more easily achieved those things as a technology executive inside large corporations.

I pursued something much more valuable to me: freedom.

It is for freedom that Christ has set us free.
Stand firm, then, and do not let yourselves be
burdened again by a yoke of slavery.

Galatians 5:1

I desired the freedom to do more of what I wanted and less of what I didn't. Freedom *from* the boredom of budgets, the insanity of status reports, and the tyranny of the tolerable that I too often experienced as an employee. And freedom *for* more time for writing and creating.

I truly believe that God planted this desire within me, the freedom to write and create, for His purposes.

I knew that if I pursued what God set in me, wholeheartedly and honestly and genuinely, the money would follow. That He would take care of my family me.

Look at the birds of the air; they do not sow or reap or
store away in barns, and yet your heavenly Father feeds
them. Are you not much more valuable than they?

Matthew 6:26

And He did take care of us, He remained our provider. I didn't always earn as much in my business as I did working for a company, especially in those early years, but I'll give up the higher income any day for the freedom and fulfillment I found.

This was my dream, my vision, my desire. And I pursued it. Wholeheartedly.

Freedom as an indie consultant doesn't mean that you won't have bosses, but that you'll be free to pick and choose those bosses, the engagements that you take on. You get to a point where you say "Yes!" when you want to and "No, thank you!" when you don't. For good reason or for no good reason at all.

This journey is life changing. When done well, the dream—the vision, the desire—pulls you forward, even effortlessly at times. It stretches you and teaches you. And grows you. It rewards you in ways that money could never comprehend.

Most of all, it grows your faith. Because, if you're a believer and you jump off that cliff, you get to a point where there's not much else to go on. And that's a beautiful thing. Maybe it's *the thing*.

You will have your own journey. It will be different than mine. The ideas, strategies, and lessons I share in this book can help you along the way. They can save you time, money, and frustration. Use it as a resource as you plan, execute, and build your own independent consulting business.

I hope *Unselling* provides encouragement and hope for you as you pursue freedom and life and experience both more abundantly.

I don't believe anything represents as giant a leap of faith as willingly and deliberately stopping income. Cold. Without knowing where the next paycheck might come from. Or when. Or if.

I did that.

And I survived. And thrived.

You can too. The pages that follow will show you how.

CHAPTER 1

Questions for Guidance and Action

1. What are your biggest fears as an independent consultant or business owner?

2. Who are you sharing these fears with? Your spouse? Close friend of faith? Accountability partner? Counselor? Business coach?

3. What promise(s) from God's Word will you write down and trust?

4. What do you want out of this journey?

5. What do you want out of your business?

6. How do you expect your business to serve your personal life?

7. What is the single biggest action you will take today to move yourself closer to a client engagement?

8. What is the next single biggest action you will take?

9. And the next?

UNSELLING NOTES

"Ma'am, there isn't a product on the
market that sucks like ours does."

CHAPTER 2

In Pursuit of Unselling

You, my brothers and sisters, were called to be free.
But do not use your freedom to indulge the flesh;
rather, serve one another humbly in love.

Galatians 5:13

~ Key Point ~

Make sales what you want and need it to be. Nothing less.
Nothing more.

Unselling 101

I'm not a salesperson. Never have been, never want to be. But I still
need to bring dollars in the door if I want to survive on my own
and achieve the freedom that I'm after.

And, so do you!

The approach I use as an introverted person to develop business
turns popular sales techniques on their head. Instead of working to
sell, I work to give. Instead of developing and remembering and

following a sales process, my process simply requires genuineness and a giving heart.

Sales is a process, nothing more. It's the process of moving a prospect from their point of pain or need to an energetic "Yes!"

There are a multitude of processes, techniques, and approaches for getting to that "Yes!"

Some approaches come across as a hard sell, wielding a bit too much pressure. The salesperson employs a heavy-handed and manipulative approach. You want to go home and take a shower after those encounters.

Some feel too soft. These are the situations where you—the buyer—are the one putting the effort into the deal, chasing the salesperson down to check on colors and styles and delivery options. You don't need a shower afterward; you need a nap.

Some approaches feel just right. Throughout the process, you're treated like a human being. You are heard and respected, as if you are an important part of the transaction. No shower, no nap, just the joy afterward of knowing that your need was understood and addressed, that your life has been enhanced because of your new widget, gadget, or thingamabob.

Sales processes can be simple or complex in their design, be easy or hard to remember, and feel natural or forced in their execution. For some reason, we humans tend toward the complex, hard, and forced, as if these attributes bring better results.

They don't.

Just because something doesn't hurt doesn't mean you're doing it wrong. For me, simple, natural, and genuine beat complex, hard, and forced any day, especially when it comes to developing business.

I discovered that it is possible to achieve great results through a simple, easy, and natural approach to "sales." My approach is simple for me to remember and easy to follow because I get to be my natural self.

You can achieve this too, even though you and I are two very different people. The hardest parts of the process are showing up and knowing what to say.

A snowball's chance

Selling a car is a transactional sale. One and done. After we sign the paperwork and hand over our firstborn, most of us never see that salesperson again.

Certainly, some salespeople put time and effort into building relationships after the sale is completed. Christmas cards, birthday cards, phone calls, allowing you to visit your firstborn. The effort is nice, but it started with a cold transaction.

That's not what we're after here.

We want a "sales" model that mimics a snowball rolling down a steep hill. We give the snowball an initial push to begin its journey. It rolls slowly at first, and then picks up speed, momentum, and size as it rolls down the hill.

Transactional sales don't behave like this. They're not sustainable, especially for indie consultants. They don't snowball into more and more *incoming* business. In fact, they don't snowball at all. They're one and done. They simply melt into a puddle. You make a sale and then have to begin the effort all over again to make the next one happen.

The other pitfall with transactional sales is that we view everyone as a prospect. If you approach business by seeking a sale with every interaction, it will sap your energy and turn people off. They'll sense that you're after a sale, that you're not actually seeking to understand whether they even have a need that you could meet.

With a transactional sales approach, over time you will experience low return for your efforts. You'll either become discouraged from the constant rejection or you'll need to become comfortable with selling your wares to people who may not even need them.

You will eventually develop a negative reputation, and soon most of your effort will go into overcoming that reputation. It just doesn't work.

We as business owners go down this path, though, because we want income. And when do we want it? *Now!*

Transactional sales will give you that quick hit of income, but over time you'll sacrifice relationships and business viability. And worse, you'll sacrifice the life that you're truly after. Transactional sales might deliver quick wins, but they don't snowball into a successful, self-sustaining business.

With an indie consulting business, you want to build a reputation where people happily and proactively refer business to you. You want the snowball to roll itself. This is what makes the phone ring and the email ding.

If you're going to succeed, you want to have a business development approach where *all* of your efforts work together and snowball into incoming business—business that finds you—with little to no sales effort on your part.

It is possible.

This sustainable approach requires developing trusted relationships within your network, which takes time. It also requires seeking ways to help others and giving of yourself first before you seek to receive. Throughout this time, you will have the opportunity to quietly and humbly weave your value proposition into each conversation, educating people in your network about you and your service.

Along the way, you will make yourself memorable not by what you get but by what you give, by what you do for others.

From the beginning of my business, I have been regularly blessed with introductions to CEOs, CFOs, COOs, and HR executives of small, medium, and even large corporations. I am always grateful and honored, and I carry that gratefulness of heart and honor throughout each engagement.

I would not have received those introductions if I simply showed up and sold something. People in my network would never have introduced me to their C-level friends because that would have broken their own trusted relationships.

If you always respect those trusted introductions by only seeking to help and give versus seeking to sell and receive, you will build a sustainable business that snowballs into the life that you desire—into the unselling life.

You will make it easy for others to refer business to you, and you'll build a reputation of being worthy of introductions. Always take care of the people that you're introduced to, no matter what it takes, even if it means a loss on the deal for you.

Do this consistently and often enough and you'll build a personal and business brand that spreads like wildfire... where the selling is done for you.

À la carte consulting

One of my favorite restaurants in the small town I grew up in was Vint's. If it could be deep fried, there's a good chance they had it.

This was the type of place where you walked in and ordered your food at the counter, then your food was wrapped in paper and set on an orange plastic tray.

The giant menu with dozens of items hung high on the wall behind the counter. Listed on their menu was the funny phrase, *à la carte*. At least it was funny to a ten-year-old boy. I asked my dad what it meant. "You can pick and choose any items from the menu that you want," he said.

Awesome! I could have fish, hush puppies, fries, and a shake? Heaven for a little boy!

À la carte works well for little boys and fast food, but not so much for building an indie consulting business.

Fast-forward that hungry little boy thirty-some years.

It was my second year out on my own. I was meeting with the president of a small company that had many challenges with technology. He invited me to his office to talk about what I do and to learn if I might have some solutions for his situation.

In our hour-long discussion, he spent just a few minutes talking about his situation and I spent rest of the time talking about all of the information technology (IT) services that I offered.

"My primary service is interim chief information officer. But I can also provide business–IT alignment services. This helps make sure that IT works on the highest-value efforts for the business. But, IT also needs to deliver projects on time and within budget, so I can implement a project management office, assess failing projects and get them back on track, or coach your project managers. Of course, there are also infrastructure issues that you need to be aware of. For example, data backups and disaster recovery. But, before we focus on any of those things, we should probably do an organizational assessment because...."

Yep, I put him through forty-five minutes of this.

It was as if I didn't hear a word he said about his needs. I had my services and was going to make sure he heard every one of them. (I certainly didn't want to miss an opportunity!) So, I described my entire à la carte menu for him. On my business website at the time, I listed three practice areas and seven services under each. That's a hefty *twenty-one* services, all from little ole John.

I was so proud that I could offer all of these options, showing how deep and broad my skills, abilities, and experiences were. Surely he would be impressed and hire me on the spot, and I would be rolling in the dough.

Instead, he said, "I'd like to hire you, but I don't know what you do."

Doh!!

I made a couple mistakes here. (OK, I made many more than a couple, but let's acknowledge John's bruised ego, start small, and focus on just a tiny subset of them.)

Looking back, twenty-one services seems so ridiculous. What was I thinking?!

Well, I was thinking that if I could tell him (and rest of the world) *every single thing* that I am capable of doing, then he simply had to tell me which of my really awesome services he wanted (the more the merrier, of course). I would neatly wrap up each one and place them on a bright orange serving tray for him.

That's not what buyers want, especially executives. They shouldn't have to be the one matching a consultant's services to their problems. That's *our* job.

But, that's what indies do when we don't want to miss an opportunity—we list our entire menu and hope the buyer can see which menu item will meet their needs.

This isn't fast food, where the buyer does all of the work to decide how to solve their hunger problem.

I never really showed that I cared about him or his needs. I didn't even express that I fully understood them!

Buyers, especially executives, definitely want solutions (the right solutions) wrapped up in a neat little package. However, it's our responsibility to do this, not theirs.

After hearing that he didn't know what I did, I quickly tried backpedaling out of the pen of pig pooh I'd created by attempting to describe his needs and expressing how I could help him. But it was too late. I had talked myself out of an opportunity.

I was certainly frustrated with myself, but I instantly saw the three biggest blunders I'd made with this executive. And those blunders proved to be a gold mine for me. They helped me to self-correct my approach to these meetings, which significantly improved my ability to gain business.

The goldmine I blundered into?

1. The more I talked, the less he heard and the more confused he became.

2. I didn't seek to fully understand him and his situation before I sought to be fully understood.

3. I put the burden of the sale on him. I forced him to determine which of my services would solve his problem.

The whole time I was blathering on, he was waiting for me to prove that I understood his problem and that I had the skills and experience to solve it. Anything less, and he wasn't interested. Anything more, and he wasn't interested.

I'm sure at some point in my rambling, I began to sound like Charlie Brown's teacher to him. "Wah wah wah wuh wah wah wah wuh wah wah wah...."

It takes time, trial, and error to thread that needle, to find that fine line between too little and too much talking. If ever in doubt, always go with less. You can always add more as the discussion goes on, but you can't put drivel back in your mouth once it's out there.

The more we say, the less people hear.

Harry Beckwith (*Selling the Invisible*, 1997)

No pain, no gain; know pain, know gain

Here's how to put your buyers and their situations first when you're seated across from them:

1. Seek to understand their current pain or opportunity. Care about them and their situation first and foremost... not your bank account balance, your mortgage payment, or the fact that you may not have enough gas to get home.

2. Acknowledge their situation by concretely, concisely, and accurately repeating it back to them.

3. Start a relationship; don't sell. Have a dialogue; don't give a presentation. *Please.* Resist the urge to sell yourself or use a slide deck. If you need a visual, make it a one-pager and print it out. Make it simple, make it interesting, make it visually appealing, and make it high-quality. Use a good mix of words and graphics that express your value, process, and differentiation.

4. Concretely and concisely express your experience in solving their specific problem—nothing else needs to be said.

5. *Do not* tell them that they have a bigger problem, even though you see it, even though it's there.

(Regarding that last point: This is a totally different topic, but it's an important one. Bottom line: you will lose the opportunity if you tell them they have a bigger problem. I know this sounds unprofessional, but trust me, it isn't. They can't see beyond their immediate problem, even if it's peripheral, tactical, or a symptom of a bigger, more strategic one that you see. Meet their current need and while you're doing that, build a relationship with them, learn their culture, and get more insights into the bigger problem. Then you'll be positioned well to be a more strategic consultant for them. This takes patience and trust, but it's the right thing to do for the client.)

If you don't seek to understand and solve their immediate pain, you won't have any gain. You'll leave your prospect continuing to search for someone who *is* willing to understand and solve it.

Playing Noah Webster

For us indies, it's important to know how the concepts of sales, marketing, and business development all interact and interrelate. The more you understand each of these concepts, the more you'll be able to minimize the time invested in the ones you don't like and spend more time on the ones you do like (or at least can tolerate).

And, no, you can't minimize all of them until they evaporate into nothingness. No one would know about you, you wouldn't create any income, and you wouldn't have a business.

Nice try....

You certainly don't need to become a sales or marketing expert. However, you *do* need to become a business development expert. (We'll talk about how to make this happen in chapter 3, and throughout the remainder of the book.)

Here's a classic yet truly simple definition of sales and marketing: marketing creates awareness, sales creates transactions.

I have good news for you though: You can play Noah Webster (known for publishing dictionaries, his first in 1806) and define sales and marketing for yourself. That's what I did, and it made all the difference in the world for me. It removed the pressure to become a salesperson, pressure that I had put on myself. Toss out what you've learned or heard about sales and marketing and have them makes sense for you and your business.

In terms of marketing, here's *my* definition for *my* indie consulting business: Marketing is the act of wasting money hoping it will do the job I should be doing, which is going out and building and growing a trusted network.

You can't win the battle of independent consulting through marketing, by tossing proxies of paper and pixels out into the world, hoping and praying clients will somehow show up. It doesn't work this way. What we do requires relationship development—real, personal, genuine relationship development.

Defining sales for yourself will be equally valuable for you. In fact, it was the most freeing strategy I discovered for my business. My definition eliminated the fears I had about selling (especially as an introvert) and allowed me to be myself and still get to that all-important "Yes!"

The five-second salesperson

I decided early in my business that sales for me was simply *that moment in time* when I was sitting across from a buyer and I plainly and confidently let them know that I'd love to work with them and asked if I could put together a draft agreement.

This was my approach to selling, reducing it to as small of a timeframe as possible, while allowing me to comfortably be myself and still close opportunities.

That's it. Nothing more.

I only had to be a "salesperson" for a few seconds. (More freedom for John!)

First, regarding my "five-second sales pitch," prospective clients want to know that you desire to work with them. You need to clearly communicate this desire. Let them know that you'd love to work with them. Don't make them wonder whether you want to. If you're not clear, they might determine on their own that you don't. Second, I've yet to have anyone tell me no, that they didn't want me to put together a draft agreement. It's a huge win for them. They don't have to worry about coming up with an agreement themselves, and they get to look at your contract language (which reveals who you are as a business person and individual) prior to making even a verbal decision. No commitment, no risk. They will appreciate you for offering this!

The fact that no one has yet turned down a draft agreement has *nothing* to do with my salesmanship (thank goodness!), but *everything* to do with all of my efforts prior to those few seconds. And much of that work occurred even before the buyer knew who I was. Pretty cool, huh?!

Why I get business

Because I'm a five-second salesperson, I don't have to be out selling. I don't cold call or knock on doors. There's nothing at all wrong with these strategies; *I'm* just not comfortable doing them, nor do I think they work for indie consultants.

There's a real talent and skill to selling, one that requires an outgoing nature, patience, and attention to process—none of which I have.

Talented salespeople are quite impressive and worth the high compensation the best of them receive. All that they do moves a prospect closer and closer to "Yes"—all that I do (as a consultant) moves a prospect closer to a *problem solved.* The salesperson's true value *ends* at "Yes," whereas an independent consultant's true value *begins* at "Yes."

I certainly wish I could skip the step of business development and just get on with solving strategic business problems. But, I freely chose the indie route, so I own it all, including the downright indispensable responsibility of creating business opportunities. There's no way around this but to put on my "biz dev" hat and create my own opportunities to solve strategic business problems.

So, if I own this responsibility and my work truly begins at yes, yet I'm not out selling, why do I still get business?

Because I want it. I want it with all my heart and soul and being. Consulting income stood between me and my desire for my *life.* And I wasn't going to let anything keep me from fulfilling that desire.

I desperately wanted consulting income, because I desperately didn't want a job. I wanted the freedom to write.

I truly believe that this is the most important reason for *why* I get business: I have a clear vision for my life and relentlessly pursue it with my whole heart.

Sales to me is an ugly and vicious orc straight out of *The Lord of the Rings.* It stood there, between me and my life's vision, hideous and horrifying, scaring me, daring me to take him on, hoping I would simply cower and retreat in fear.

But, I didn't. The desire to write full time was bigger than my fears. Strike that. My God, the one who created me, is bigger than my fears. I leaned on Him and trusted Him more and more to help me survive out in the cruel, cruel world of independent consulting.

> *I can do all things through him who gives me strength.*
>
> Philippians 4:13

We can, and need to, absolutely trust in God to overcome our fears.

The difference between the how and the why

Understanding *how* you get business—the strategies and mechanics of business development—and continually perfecting it will keep you in the game financially. Understanding *why* you get business—knowing the essence of who you are and the life that you desire—will keep you in the game emotionally.

It's way easier to be who we are naturally and pursue something beyond money and material things than to put in the effort to be someone else and pursue what the world values. Those in your network will recognize when you're being genuine and when you're not. People want to be around genuine people, and they truly desire to refer business to them.

The bulk of *Unselling*, including the strategies in this chapter, describes how I get business. But I can't write about *the how* without emphasizing *the why*. Never lose sight of the fact that there's an underlying drive in you for something greater than the business itself. This underlying drive has nothing to do with business at all—it is your *why*. When you know your *why*, and *resolutely pursue it*, you'll find the determination to build and continually improve *the how*.

Unselling—the definition

What exactly is unselling?

Unselling is that point in your indie consulting life when you've built such a powerful business development engine that opportunities are pouring in from every direction, but you're ready to say no, to shift from business to life, to the life that you truly desire.

The first time I stepped into this unselling life I wasn't even aware of what was happening; I wasn't ready. In my first opportunity, I failed at unselling. I told a CFO no to the interim CIO consulting role that she offered me. But, she persisted. Adamantly. I eventually said yes. I thoroughly enjoyed the client and engagement, but I knew it would be my last.

The second time I stepped into unselling mode I was ready. I was referred to a CEO and he wanted to hire me as their interim CIO. I said no. He came back two more times asking me to take the assignment. I said no two more times, and explained why I was saying no. He finally gave in. "I heard you," he said, "I just wanted to make sure you were consistent."

I loved that feeling of turning down business, literally leaving income on the table (income into the six figures). I desired something more than income; I desired freedom. Saying no felt like pure freedom.

Stepping into unselling mode meant that I had built a successful independent consulting business (without selling), and I could now reap the benefits and pursue the life I truly desired.

Part of that freedom was shifting my business from full-time consulting and interim management to CIO executive search (which I could do from anywhere). This business model would also give me more time to write. I don't go to an office. I work out of my house or in a coffee shop or from wherever I choose. I don't worry about how many engagements I have or when they'll show up. I trust that they will, and they do. And I get to balance the freedom to work with the freedom to write, with the freedom for life with my family and friends, with the freedom to help others.

Unselling is also irony at its best. In the beginning you're begging for business when you most need it. And then, when you don't need it or even want it, it floods in.

Pretty sweet irony, if you ask me.

The twelve-plus years that I put into developing my network and business brought me to the life I desired—a life of freedom, of working less ,and living more.

What type of life would unselling bring to you?

In the next chapter we'll look at business development and building the indie engine to get you there.

CHAPTER 2

Questions for Guidance and Action

1. What will sales be to you? What is your definition of sales?

2. Why will you get business? What will keep you emotionally motivated?

3. What would an unselling life look like to you?

4. What primary service will you provide/do you want to be known for?

5. What is the single biggest action you will take today to move yourself closer to a client engagement?

6. What is the next single biggest action you will take?

7. And the next?

UNSELLING NOTES

"They normally sell for $2 each, but if you buy before we reach the sidewalk, I can let the entire box go for $21.95."

CHAPTER 3

Starting Your Indie Engine

A good name is more desirable than great riches;
to be esteemed is better than silver or gold.

Proverbs 22:1

~ Key Point ~

Developing business isn't about selling, it's about serving.

The indie engine

We make a living by what we get, but
we make a life by what we give.

Winston Churchill

While I love this Churchill quote, I believe you can make a life *and* earn a living by what you give.

The core or "glue" of my business development engine is based on just that: giving, helping, and serving others. But, there's more to developing business than just the giving. There are other important components and actions that most indies fail to do or aren't persistent or consistent with.

Here are the components of my indie business development engine:

1. Networking

2. Helping and educating

3. Marketing

4. Speaking and writing

5. Serving clients

I'll give a brief overview of the five components, and then we'll dig deep into each one in the remaining chapters.

1. Networking

Networking is simply the continual act of meeting new people and staying in touch with those already in your network, all with the primary purpose of educating them about your business and seeking opportunities to help and give.

Networking is foundational to your success, especially early in your business. It will make you or break you. The more you're out of your office and in front of people, the greater your chance of success.

2. Helping and educating

Helping and educating go together like bacon and eggs, chips and salsa, peanut butter and bananas. They're each quite awesome by themselves, but oh, so much better together.

Helping can be most any type of assistance you can think of—providing referrals, making introductions, helping someone find a job, editing a résumé, reviewing a blog posting, collaborating on a business idea, and on and on. Be an open resource for people in your network. Use your talents, time, resources, experiences, expertise, and insights for the benefit of others. You will be appreciated… and remembered.

"…It is more blessed to give than to receive."

Acts 20:35

Helping others does come back to you, as "[a] good measure, pressed down, shaken together and running over" (Luke 6:38). And, for some reason, Luke adds that it will then be poured into your lap. You might want to have a large bucket ready!

This is exactly what I experienced. It worked because it was natural and genuine for me to help and give. This concept, way more than any other, allowed me to be myself, generate an income far above average, and eventually achieve the freedom I desired.

If helping is the content of your book (the amount of time you spend focused on the other person in a networking situation), then educating is the back cover (the amount of time you spend focused on yourself and your business).

It's that short.

Not only short, educating needs to be clear, relatable, and memorable. The best way to be clear, relatable, and memorable is through stories.

Here's an example of a story an indie project manager might share:

"Have you ever experienced a software project failure? It's kind of like watching a train wreck in slow motion. Everyone sees it happening. They hear the train whistle blow, the wheels squealing on the tracks, the train cars banging into each other, and maybe even a scream or two. In the end, there's nothing left but a giant pile of twisted metal. This doesn't have

to happen. I know how to save those projects from becoming a train wreck. I've saved dozens of them. The last one was a software implementation project for an insurance company. I identified the major issues for the client, recommended some changes, and then helped them implement those changes. We got the project back on track for a successful delivery. What took nine months to fail, we completed in six. If you hear of a company in this situation, I would welcome an introduction, I would love to help them."

If you can't succinctly and memorably articulate what you do, how do you expect people in your network to remember you, remember what you do, and articulate it to others? Your indie business will be just another train wreck in slow motion.

Make it easy for others to remember you and what you do, and they will make business development easy for you.

3. Marketing

Marketing is one big can of worms, filled with more big cans of worms. (Yes, it's that big of a can!) Fun and exciting if you're a worm farmer, a bit dirty and slimy for the rest of us.

Where selling is typically one-to-one messaging with the sole intent of creating a transaction, marketing is one-to-many messaging. You're creating awareness of your brand, product, or service to the masses.

Think TV commercials, pop-up ads on websites, magazine ads, spam email, billboards, brand logos on golf balls and race cars, product placements in movies and TV shows, even those business cards and flyers stacked on top of each other on the bulletin board of your local coffee shop.

Marketing options for businesses are endless, but they often prove costly, especially for indie consultants.

Chapter 6 dares to open this can of worms, and we'll even let a few squirm around in our hands.

4. Speaking and writing

For some reason, speaking is like a holy grail for independent consultants. I understand why, but it rarely works out as expected.

What you expect: You speak to a group of people (somewhere between two and 200), and you have this vision that, after the fifteen minutes of applause slows, they'll be knocking each other over trying to be the first to talk with you about your brilliance. "And, oh, can you come in and consult with us full-time for six months starting tomorrow?"

How it actually works: You finish speaking. Two of the seven people in the room come up to you and let you know they enjoyed your presentation. These are the people with high empathy. Your speech wasn't that great and they didn't get much out of it, but they want to make you feel good about yourself. There is one person, however, who is interested in maybe having you help their company. You exchange business cards and never see each other again.

I'm not bemoaning the reality of speaking at all, just setting proper expectations.

The bottom line: to effectively leverage speaking and writing for your business, you need to be entertaining. You have a much better chance of getting business if you performed an awesome magic show… said your tagline at the end… and then gave everyone twenty minutes of their life back. *That* would be memorable!

5. Serving clients

Bragging about your endless talents and abilities to your network will move you a full yard down the field toward your goal line. (You started at your own one-yard line.) Clients bragging about you will move you the other ninety-eight yards.

There's no better way to develop business than by serving and pleasing clients, and then letting them brag about you. Wildly successful client engagements bring all of your business development efforts full circle—they prove to your network that you are who you say you are and can do what you say you can do.

6. In summary...

Networking, helping, and educating all allow you to build your very own *extended sales force*—essentially anyone in your professional network who has the opportunity, ability, and wherewithal to refer business to you.

Marketing, speaking, and writing all bolster your networking, helping, and educating—*if* they are done well and at the right time.

Serving clients well brings your indie business full circle, and propels you forward and toward the unselling life.

Working together, these five components of the business development engine allow you to stay top of mind with your network. When anyone hears of a need they believe you can fill, you will be the first (and hopefully only) person they think of and recommend. If you've built a solid business development engine and actively keep it humming, you will be.

Chasing leads

I don't like the idea of traditional selling, especially for indie consultants. A key component of traditional selling is building a sales pipeline, and pipelines are made up of leads—*possible* opportunities that *might* produce business.

I don't chase leads; I chase relationships.

I would much prefer to meet and educate people about my value proposition, which in my mind is like planting lots and lots of seeds throughout my network, and then cultivating them until they're ready to bloom—*in their own time*. The more seeds I plant (the more people in my network that I've educated and helped), the more chance I have of something sprouting and turning into business—*business that came to me without my doing any selling at all.*

I believe a lead is an opportunity that could just as easily become a rabbit hole. Leads consume a lot of time qualifying (determining if they can actually produce income), and they require more time selling than my five-second limit. I want more freedom and time for doing the things I enjoy. So, I choose to network and educate, and let the leads chase me. If I miss opportunities because of this approach, I'm OK with that. I'm trading a little income for more freedom.

Identifying your referral network

Before you can build your engine, you need to answer two foundational questions:

1. Who is your buyer?

2. Who does your buyer trust?

These questions are important to answer. Your engine won't work without clear answers.

Who is your buyer?

Your buyer is the person inside a company, or inside a household if your business is consumer based, who (a) understands that there is a problem or opportunity/who feels the pain, (b) agrees the problem is real and needs to be solved, and (c) has the authority to say "Yes" and write a check.

Technically, this is called qualifying a lead or opportunity. With my approach to business development, however, I don't focus on leads or opportunities or on qualifying them. *I focus on relationships* within my network. However, I still need to know who my primary buyer is.

Traditional salespeople care about qualifying leads. The sooner they can qualify a lead—know for certain that it's a real problem understood by a real person with authority to make a real decision and able to write a real check—the more confident they can be in spending valuable time and money leading that prospect to a "Yes."

They also want as many leads in their sales pipeline as possible. This increases their chances of finding the best close opportunities and finding the highest profit ones, as well.

There's always some degree of qualifying needed, but with a business development model where you focus on building relationships versus building a sales pipeline, you will have buyers coming to you instead of having to push—or *sell*—your services to them. Why? Because you were referred to them by someone they trust. The client has already qualified themselves by contacting you.

The only qualifying you will need to do is determine whether it is a good opportunity for you. Is it the right industry, right project, right client, right duration, right location, etc.?

Pursuing relationships versus leads has allowed me to be who I am. I get to spend more time doing the things I want to do (networking, helping, consulting), and no time on things I don't want to do (cold calling, chasing leads, managing a sales pipeline, trying to follow a sales process).

During the first eleven years of my business, my main consulting service was interim CIO. (Of course, that was *after* I eliminated the other 20 services from my overstuffed repertoire.) As an interim management executive, I performed the role of a client's CIO as if I were a full-time employee. Most CIOs report to either the CEO or CFO of a company—it's these business leaders who most experience the pain I make go away. So, the CEO and CFO were my *primary buyers*.

Who is your primary buyer? Who is most impacted by the problem that you solve? Who has the authority to hire you and pay you to solve this problem?

You don't need to know their name, but you do need to identify the role or title they typically hold.

Who does your buyer trust?

Knowing who your buyer trusts will tell you who will be in your referral network. Anyone can be in your network, but your *referral network* is made up of those individuals who are active networkers themselves, who generously refer business to others, and who are trusted by your buyers.

I always picture my buyer, a CEO or CFO, standing surrounded by a circle of people—their most trusted advisors (my referral partners). These are the individuals they turn to when needing guidance and advice. For example, when they need to hire a consultant to solve a big strategic problem, they ask their trusted advisors who they would recommend.

You want to be connected to—by actively *networking* with—as many of these trusted advisors as possible so that you're then connected to as many of your buyers as possible. You don't need to know the buyer, and you won't need to cold call them, spam them, stalk them, or spend countless hours and dollars begging for introductions to them. However, you *do* need to know their trusted advisors, and you need to know them well. You also need to understand the services of those trusted advisors so you can refer business to them whenever possible (actively *help* them). You also need to ensure that they know you and your services just as well (actively *educate* them).

You want to be the person that this circle of trust knows and remembers for the services that you offer. And the only way they will know and remember you is if they've had the opportunity to meet you, clearly understand what you do, trust you, and are continually reminded that you exist.

My primary referral partners are other management consultants, leadership development consultants, executive coaches, and human resources executives. I wanted to meet and help as many of these individuals as I could. I also needed to make sure that they clearly understood the problem that I solved and knew how to listen for it.

Identify your own referral network and seek with all of your might to *continually* meet, stay connected with, help, and educate as many of them as you can.

While you want to meet, help, and educate everyone, you especially want to do this with your referral network, because they are the ones with direct access to your buyer.

The drumbeat of your business

I had a professor in college who used to say, "If you can't write your idea on the back of a business card, then you don't have a clear idea."

Can you write your value proposition, your drumbeat, on the back of business card? Go ahead, give it a try. I'll wait.

How did you do?

Not easy, is it? It took me about three years to get there. It will help (tremendously) and save you a lot of frustration if you can nail this a bit faster than three years.

Your drumbeat needs to be concise. And not only concise, it needs to be clear and repeatable so that those in your network can remember it *and* repeat it.

This isn't an "elevator pitch," where you theoretically run into your ideal client on an elevator and you have 30 seconds to give your best pitch and get the meeting or you blow it and miss the opportunity of a lifetime. Elevator pitches are valuable in those settings where you have at most a minute or two to communicate your value.

A drumbeat is different and is much more valuable than an elevator pitch. It encapsulates and accentuates all of your messaging in a concise and memorable phrase.

I call it a drumbeat because that's how I see it in my head. I'm standing behind a big kettle drum (which I've honestly never done) and holding a drumstick (or timpani mallet—had to look that one up) in each hand. With deft timing and rhythm, I start beating the drum, clearly, precisely—the same note over and over. And I don't stop. I don't change the rhythm or the note—that note is my message. I'm consistent with it. I repeat it to everyone I meet. Sometimes I don't get the opportunity to do any education with an individual, but I do make sure that I share my drumbeat.

This micro-commercial will be the drumbeat of your message to your network and to the world. It will support and enhance your education, marketing, speaking, and writing.

My drumbeat was, "I'm an interim CIO. I fix broken IT organizations."

This drumbeat is clear, concise, relatable, and memorable. Yours should be as well.

Most people I met with had experienced IT organizations, both the awesome kind and the not-so-awesome kind, so they could relate to the drumbeat, and nodded their head in understanding.

People in your network are trying to remember hundreds or even thousands of other people that they know, not just you (even though you are very awesome and special). You get one little neuron in their brain in which to implant your message. Use it wisely. Make it easy for them to remember you by crafting a drumbeat that is clear, concise, relatable, and memorable.

I know consultants who say, "I'm a strategic problem solver."

This message might be concise, but it's not clear. Or relatable. Or memorable.

Please don't be a strategic anything. The word strategic means too many things to too many people. It's way too open to interpretation. You'll spend your time explaining what you mean by strategic and probably put the person sitting across from you into a strategic slumber.

Instead, steal from a friend of mine who tells people, "I'm an independent marketing executive. I bring cash in the door."

I want to hire her!

Here's another popular, yet ineffective message: "I'm a project manager."

I'm sure you are, but so are 20 million other people in the world. Why would those in your network remember you over the other 19,999,999 project managers, at least a few dozen or few hundred of whom are competing against you?

To be fair, "project manager" is better than "strategic problem solver." But, it's still a bit boring and not distinguishable or memorable.

Instead, be "an independent project manager who consistently implements software projects on time and within budget," or, "an independent project leader who knows how to roll out marketing campaigns against all odds."

Yes, you *might* miss opportunities that aren't software or marketing related, but you will be remembered for software or marketing opportunities.

Developing a clear, concise, relatable, and memorable message isn't easy. We make it difficult because we try to write one that encompasses all that we're capable of doing. We end up crafting one that is convoluted or generic. Either way, we're trying to be all things to all people so that we don't miss any opportunities (to make money). But, instead of being all things to all people, we end up being nothing to everyone. (Remember my twenty-one services and the executive who said he'd like to hire me but didn't know what I did?)

If your *ideal* engagement came wrapped as a Christmas gift and set before you—dressed to the nines with shiny paper, red ribbon, and bow—what would be inside? What exactly would you be doing as a consultant, and for what type of client? What difference would you make for them?

I want an official Red Ryder, carbine action, two-hundred shot range model air rifle with a compass in the stock and this thing that tells time!

Ralphie Parker in
A Christmas Story (MGM, 1983)

Now that's specific!

If you try to incorporate more than a single purpose in your drumbeat, you will miss a lot of opportunities because no one will have a clear idea of what you're seeking. They won't know when to recognize an opportunity that you can help solve, and they won't be able to play matchmaker for you.

Drumbeats that are clear, concise, and relatable are powerful for indies. They help make you memorable; they help you stand out in a crowded and ever-growing consulting space.

But wait, there's more!

Something awesome happened when I went narrow with my message. In addition to increasing the number of interim CIO referrals, I also received referrals for other IT-related work. A lot of referrals.

Most of these I couldn't take on or didn't want to take on. I didn't ignore them, though. I gave them away. I referred them to other indies in my network and to larger consulting firms. Why? Because I still wanted to help the company in need, and I also wanted to help other consultants, whether a fellow indie or a larger firm.

Helping others connects us and ties us together. The more we give, the more opportunity there is to receive. I don't focus on the receiving though. That will happen. It *has* happened for me non-stop for several years now. Instead of focusing on the receiving, I continually seek out opportunities to help and give, and nothing is better than giving income-producing referrals to others.

Many of the people I referred business to reciprocated the generosity with referrals back to me. Some never did, though, and that's more than OK. I never kept score. Relationships aren't about keeping score—who's up or down, who's winning or losing, or who's in my dog house. I simply love stoking the fires of success for other independent consultants. I know what it means for them: not just the revenue, but the freedom of living the life they deeply desire.

What's the key takeaway here? Being very narrow in your quest for consulting work will get you exactly the type of work you're seeking. The more specific and memorable of a drumbeat you can craft, the more success you'll have. As a bonus, your well-crafted, precise drumbeat will bring you additional, somewhat peripheral, opportunities as well. These opportunities will be valuable for you in serving your network and rewarding your extended "sales force."

After all, developing business isn't about selling, but about serving.

CHAPTER 3

Questions for Guidance and Action

1. Who is your primary buyer inside a company (by title or role)?

2. Who does your primary buyer trust/turn to when they need help? (These types of individuals become your trusted referral network.)

3. What is your drumbeat message (at least in draft form)?

4. What is the single biggest action you will take today to move yourself closer to a client engagement?

5. What is the next single biggest action you will take?

6. And the next?

UNSELLING NOTES

"It looks like we're the first ones here."

CHAPTER 4

The Joy of Networking

Each of you should use whatever gift you have received to serve others, as faithful stewards of God's grace in its various forms.

1 Peter 4:10

~ Key Point ~

Networking isn't about meeting as many people as possible, but about getting to *know* and *helping* as many people as possible.

Spoiler alert!

In the movie *Leap Year* (Universal Pictures, 2010) there's a scene near the end where the main character, Anna (played by Amy Adams), purposefully sets off the fire alarm of the highly coveted apartment she and her fiancé (Jeremy) just moved into. It was a test. Anna wanted to see what Jeremy would take as they escaped—what he valued most.

He grabs his phone, laptop, and video camera—gadgets and things. Not quite so concerned about Anna.

The spoiler alert isn't in case you haven't seen the movie. It's in case you have the notion that you'll be able to create income by only grabbing and spending time with gadgets and things, instead of spending time with people.

If you're starting an indie consulting business—or any business where you'll rely heavily on referrals from other people—you won't have the luxury of starting with an income stream, so the *only* thing you should be grabbing are human beings.

If you're an introvert, the biggest mistake you'll make in the beginning is hiding behind your desk, staring at your computer screen, begging for your phone to ring while doing anything and everything except getting out and meeting people. You'll spend your day writing articles and blogs. You'll finally start that book you've always wanted to write. You'll go to staples.com to stock up on critical office supplies (especially those colored sticky notes shaped like hearts). You'll spend hours researching companies in your city. You'll spend time documenting those processes so critical to serving your clients (if you ever get any). You'll create a detailed strategic plan for growing and expanding your business. You'll even waste time reading books on business development and networking. (No, wait! Do that one!)

Excuses. All of them.

You will waste your time.

And lose ground.

You will not find clients through your keyboard.

You can't.

I've tried.

If you're the introverted and creative type, you'll spend weeks designing your logo, website, and business cards. You'll open up your word processing software and design marketing fliers. You are certain that once the world sees them, clients will be beating down your door to hire you.

The problem is, they won't see them. Or hire you.

You will use every excuse imaginable to grab anything, as long as it's not a living, breathing human being.

I know, because I've done all of these things. And failed.

So, here we sit, between the comfort of how God wired us and the drive to have our own business.

Something has to give.

In year two of my flailing indie consulting business I hired an entrepreneur coach—Lenora. Here's a snippet from our first conversation:

"How are you planning to develop business?" Lenora asked me.

"I'm not a salesperson, so I'm not out cold calling or knocking on doors," I responded.

"OK, but how do you plan to develop business, you know, find clients and create income?"

"I'd like to write a book and then use that to market myself."

[Insert image of Lenora laughing. Out loud. In a crowded coffee shop.]

"No, you're not going to write a book," she said, still laughing.

[Insert image of John shocked by Lenora's moxie for telling him, her client, no.]

"Why not?" I asked.

"Because you need clients and you won't find them sitting behind a computer, writing."

"OK, then, I'll hire someone to develop business for me so I can write."

"No. You're not going to hire someone to develop business for you."

[Lenora likes to say no a lot.]

"What? Why not?!" I demanded.

"Because you have to learn how to do your own business development before you can teach someone else to do it."

[John's shocked look turns to a scowl.]

"But, what if I...."

"No," she said.

[More scowling.]
[Lenora didn't budget, and I didn't start that book for three years.]

I knew Lenora was right, but I held to the misguided belief that I could simply do what I wanted to do (write) and that would somehow bring me clients and income. It's a silly notion, I know, but I desperately wanted to believe it. However, even more desperately, I wanted to make it on my own. So, I faced the cold, hard fact that I needed to be out meeting and talking with people. People who could introduce me to clients. Clients with strategic problems. And with a checkbook.

After that conversation with Lenora, I went on a networking frenzy. A mission. Lenora introduced me to several people, and they in turn introduced me to even more people. I also sought out and attended countless networking groups and events.

My network expanded. Rapidly.

That frenzy lasted several years, and my network grew by a couple thousand people. Real, in-the-flesh people. Not just names and faces and profiles on a social media site. Real people. I shook their hands. Heard their stories. Learned their needs.

Lenora was right twelve years ago, and she's still right today. Until we have sustainable business income, we simply cannot hide behind writing, or marketing, or a website, or documenting processes, or another person, and think these will bring us business. They won't. It's only after we've built out our network and stream of incoming referrals that we've positioned ourselves to effectively leverage these broader growth strategies.

People buy strategic services through trusted people—not from books, or blogs, or websites, or marketing fliers, or processes. We need to be out meeting with people face-to-face. We need to do the hard work of networking, both one-on-one and through organizations and events.

On the other end of the spectrum, if you're an extrovert, you will naturally want to be out there talking with people. With anyone who will listen. For as long as they will listen.

Good for you!

Your danger as an extroverted independent consultant, however, will be believing that you can jump into networking and people will immediately refer business to you.

In the world of independent consulting, we first need to establish relationships and trust before others will be open to referring business to us. Building trust takes time, and this requires listening, caring, giving, and getting to know people. That's *our* job, whether we're introverted, extroverted, somewhere in between, don't know, or don't care. You and I are the ones seeking the business, so we need to take the lead in listening, understanding, caring, giving, and getting to know others.

This is the essence of what it takes to build a successful, growing, self-sustaining indie consulting business without selling.

One-on-one networking

At its simplest level, networking is two people meeting for a coffee (or tea, or lunch, or breakfast, or even just a walk) with the intent of understanding each other's primary need and then offering to help meet those needs, when possible.

The more specific and clear you are about your need, the easier you make it for the other person to help you. Your primary need is for referrals to consulting opportunities.

You want the people you meet to know you and to remember you and your drumbeat. That way, you'll be front and center in their minds when anyone in their network has a need that you might be able to fill.

You won't be a good fit for all of the needs your network refers to you. Take on the ones you can be successful doing and decline the rest... or refer them to other indies in your network.

People will be very hesitant to refer you (extend their credibility to someone in their network) until they know you and trust you. The fastest way to get there, however, is by *seeking to know and trust them first.*

As an indie, the types of needs that you'll hear from people in your network will run deep and wide, from helping with a job search to helping with a candidate search, from requests for consulting referrals to requests for introductions to people in your network.

Jumpstart your network

If you are building a professional network from scratch, contacting everyone who already knows you and trusts you is the best way to get started.

Here's an easy process to follow for doing just this:

Walk through the last five to ten years of your career and write down each company you worked for and the unique positions that you held in each one. Then, walk back through each position and write down the names of at least five people who saw you for the talent you are. These are the people who know you already and might recommend you to others or even refer business to you. Challenge yourself to come up with twenty names, or thirty, or more! You can then include family and friends on your list if you think they may be able to assist you in jumpstarting your network.

Do not be afraid to include on your list people who were higher up in the organization, even if at the VP, SVP, CXO, or even board level. (I recommend only reaching out to individuals in this group if you've personally met them, though.) Most people, not everyone, at this level tend to have a passion for wanting to help others with their careers and business ventures. These are also the individuals who can make valuable introductions for you.

Next, reach out to each of them (email or LinkedIn messages are usually best) and let them know what you're seeking.

"I'm launching my own independent consulting business, and one of my first steps is to reconnect with people that I've worked with in the past. I'd like to share with you what my focus will be, get your feedback on my plans, and see if you might know of others I should meet. I would also enjoy hearing how you're doing."

While not everyone will accept your invitation, you will be surprised that the majority are very open to meeting with you and helping you however they can.

Schedule a time for coffee, tea, breakfast, lunch, dinner—whatever works best for *them*. Make the date, time, and location convenient for them as well.

Follow up with a meeting notice. And then a day or two before your meeting, send a brief email (or text or phone call, if appropriate) confirming the time and location and letting them know you're looking forward to getting together.

Prior to the day of the meeting, prepare your topics and questions, and review your drumbeat (at least in draft mode).

During the meeting, listen more than you talk. Be clear and concise with your business model and drumbeat. Get their feedback, insights, and guidance. Be humble and gracious.

Remember to ask for an update on their career and life, and definitely ask them if there's anything that you might be able to help them with!

Finally, follow up with a thank you note and a list of items they offered to help with, and the list you offered to help them with.

Here are the three most important questions to ask your networking partners:

1. I am interested in meeting [*insert the types of people who are in your referral network*]. Is there anyone in your network

who would be a good connection for me that you would be willing to introduce me to?

2. If you hear of anyone needing a [*insert your drumbeat, or a form of it*], I would welcome an introduction.

3. Is there anything that I might be able to help you with? I would welcome the opportunity to help you however I can.

Ideally, you're after introductions to your primary buyer and consulting opportunities, but honestly, that rarely happens in these situations. So, secondarily, seek introductions to those who are your referral partners. Another good introduction to seek out are those who have successful independent consulting careers in your city. They make great mentors and connectors.

This strategy also works if you have an established network but wish to grow it. (And it works great for jumpstarting a job search as well.)

Set a goal for the number of one-on-one networking meetings you wish to schedule each week and plug away until you meet that weekly goal. Five is a good, safe number; ten is a good stretch goal; more than this, and you're on your way to overachiever!

You won't be able to maintain more than five per week for very long (because you'll be busy with clients!), but you will definitely jumpstart your network.

Throughout your networking conversations, watch facial reactions as you speak. Are they nodding in understanding or agreement, or are they wincing in pain? If they're wincing, dig into why. This is great feedback for your business model, consulting focus, and messaging. Seek to hone in on what resonates with them and what doesn't.

Work to continually get better at every aspect of your networking, especially how you describe your service and drumbeat.

I promise that your network will catch fire and, because these are individuals who already know you and trust you, it will also jumpstart your income. You'll regret not having done this sooner!

Group networking

Another way to jumpstart your network is through industry networking groups and events. Most groups hold monthly meetings, either in the early morning or evening. There's something for everyone, especially in larger cities.

Networking groups exist for specific industries and for roles within companies. You'll find groups for anything and everything—from accounting and finance to recruiting and human resources, and from manufacturing and construction to technology and project management.

Here is just a small sampling of industry networking groups:

- Association for Corporate Growth (ACG)

- Project Management Institute (PMI)

- Society for Information Management (SIM)

- National Council of Nonprofits

- Chambers of Commerce

- Business Network International (BNI), whose motto is "givers gain"

- Rotary, Kiwanis, and other service-oriented networking organizations

I attended a wide variety of industry networking meetings for more than ten years. Some I attended only once; others I attended regularly for years.

Initially I showed up at these events hoping for business. When that didn't happen, I started showing up hoping to meet someone who could refer business to me that night. That didn't happen either, so I started showing up hoping to meet good referral partners. When that proved slow, I eventually just started showing up. Period. Without any expectations.

The right connections will come, but it does take time. You'll kiss a lot of frogs before you find the right referral partners. The more you can simply relax and enjoy networking events, trusting that the right referral partners will show up at the right time, the more you will enjoy those events and not experience frustration or burnout.

If you're a starving indie, you'll feel the desperation and frustration. Don't let it keep you from events or from one-on-one networking. If you withdraw from networking, you will cut yourself off from opportunities and doom your indie business.

Have I not commanded you? Be strong and courageous.
Do not be afraid; do not be discouraged, for the Lord
your God will be with you wherever you go.

Joshua 1:9

Now I rarely show up at networking meetings or events. I have a deep network that I stay in touch with, that I continue to help and educate. My network has taken on a life of its own—continuing to grow organically without much effort.

Now when I do go to networking events it's purely to see old friends and meet new ones, or to hear a particular speaker or topic that interests me. Networking is now a joy—no anxieties or expectations—it no longer feels like a chore. I don't have an agenda except to hang out and have fun with friends.

Don't let them see you sweat!

The number one rule when attending these events? Don't be desperate. Don't give even the slightest appearance of desperation. Behave like your cup is overflowing with business. Be grateful for just being there. Be curious about people and their needs. Ask them what their story is, why they're there. Show interest in them. Your goal is to build relationships, not sell.

Networking at these types of meetings can be a bit tricky, not to mention stressful—especially if you're a wallflower, like me.

Here are my keys to networking *success*: have fun, be yourself, be authentically curious about other people, have zero expectations. Good things *will* happen for you, but if you set the expectation at zero, you'll take the pressure off, relax, and be able to better connect with others.

And here are my keys to networking *frustration and failure*: expecting to find your buyers there, expecting to walk away with business, expecting *anything* except to have fun and meet some cool people. Your buyers won't be there. You won't walk away with business. Whatever you expect to happen, won't.

Who *will* be there? Interesting and fun people, and a few boring ones. (Don't be one of those.) And lots of indie business owners, consultants, and business development people.

Ask millions of questions to get to know others, and you'll do fine.

And if you end up being a wallflower, don't worry about it. Celebrate the fact that you're there holding up a wall, instead of at home holding down your couch. And with each subsequent networking meeting, you're another step closer to a bigger network, more clients, and the life that you're after.

So, grab your drink and plate of crackers and cheese, and go hold up that wall!

Start your own group

If after several months you're not finding the type of networking group you're after, consider starting your own. Such *private* networking groups exist in every city. I have been part of a couple of them. They can work really well, especially those that can sustain themselves with a consistent group over several years.

Some keys to success of private groups are:

- Have just one representative per industry/service (e.g., one real estate agent, one CPA, one executive search firm)

- Make membership by invitation only, with the full group or a leadership subset making the ultimate decision

- Don't charge a fee, unless the fee goes toward facility rental and/or food service for the meetings

- Meet consistently and ensure members attend consistently

- Set clear expectations for the purpose of the group, and of individual members

- Continually ensure that members are focused on giving and not on receiving

- Don't force referrals, allow them to happen naturally

- Maintain a long-term view—expect the group to take a couple years to gel and flow well

If you go the private group route, start small and slow. Initially, invite just two or three people to join that you know well and are certain to be strong contributing members. Solidify your small group, its purpose, and flow of meetings before you add more members. It's easier to add the right individuals at the right time than to uninvite members who aren't fitting in.

The power of compound networking

If I gave you a penny today, and then doubled that number of pennies every day for the next thirty days, do you know how much money you would have?

Try $10,737,418.20! (Go ahead, do the math.) I'm not going to promise that you'll meet 10.7 million new people in the next thirty days (which would be everyone in New York City, San Diego, and Columbus, Ohio combined), but I can promise that you will rapidly grow your network if you consistently invest your time in truly getting to know people.

With your individual network already taking off, your group networking will grow it even faster. You will soon experience the power of compound networking—like the power of compound interest (making money on money you didn't previously have)— you will meet people through people you previously didn't know.

Patience

Building trust with people takes time. It also takes time for someone to hear about an opportunity that would be a fit for you.

I've met people once, and then didn't hear from them for two or three years. Then, out of the blue, I'd get a referral from them. And I've done the same thing for others.

Be patient. Focus on serving others, and don't focus on what others can do for you.

You are planting seeds. Keep planting. Don't stop. And smile. A lot. As if you are already the busiest consultant on earth. You should be, with all of the networking you've been doing!

Reach out and touch someone

Stay in touch with people in your network. Follow up. Stay close. Be the most active member of your network. This will create opportunities for you to help and educate others, as well as create consulting opportunities for yourself.

I can't tell you how enriching being a part of this indie consulting world has been for me. It will be for you, too. It's been as personally rewarding as it has been professionally. My personal life is more fulfilling because of the people I've met through business networking.

Un-networking

I'm now at a point in my business life where I rarely go to networking events. I just don't need to. I'm more like a social possum than a social butterfly, so I go only when it will fill me and not drain me. I've gravitated to my natural state of being, which is sticking to one-on-one networking (and a lot of it). I've paid my price of admission and can now be picky about the events I attend.

You can get there, too. That point where networking is no longer a *have to go* but a *want to go.* Where you can be very choosey about the events you attend because you've put in the hard work of building a highly-effective network, especially an effective referral network. You slip from the dread of networking to the joy of it, from being dragged in kicking and screaming, to skipping in like a giddy little kid.

Your extended sales force—your very own force of nature

Through all of this networking, helping, and educating, you are building your very own *extended sales force.* Treat it well, and it will treat you well. Grow it by serving others and it will grow you. And seek to be a very active part of everyone else's extended salesforce.

This simply means listening for consulting opportunities for other indies in your network and being open and willing to refer those opportunities to them.

Do to others as you would have them do to you.

Luke 6:31

To know me is to love me

Remember that networking isn't about meeting as many people as possible. It's not a numbers game. It won't translate into more business for you.

Networking is about getting to *know* and *helping* as many people as possible. The more we know others, truly know them, the better we'll be able to help and serve them. And knowing someone is one of the greatest gifts we can give another human being.

Now, let's dive deep into the next part of the engine, *helping and educating.*

CHAPTER 4

Questions for Guidance and Action

1. a) What actions are you going to take to jumpstart/grow your network?

   b) What ten people can you reconnect with who've experienced your talents and abilities?

   c) What five networking organizations or events can you begin to attend?

   d) What networking organizations exist that are specific to your industry/area of focus?

2. Who might serve as a mentor for you on this journey?

3. What is the single biggest action you will take today to move yourself closer to a client engagement?

4. What is the next single biggest action you will take?

5. And the next?

UNSELLING NOTES

*In order to understand my business and all of my services,
you'll need to know a little about me. Now, I've only
traced my roots back to 1650, so we'll need to start there.*

CHAPTER 5

Helping and Educating

Remember this: Whoever sows sparingly
will also reap sparingly, and whoever sows
generously will also reap generously.

2 Corinthians 9:6

~ Key Point ~

Helping and educating are the seeds of indie business success.

How it's done

About three years into my consulting business, I created a leadership development program for technology leaders. I love coaching and developing people, so this program would allow me to invest in up-and-coming technology leaders.

The members signed up for a year at a time, paying a modest annual fee. We met every month for a half-day, walking through leadership concepts and discussing their work challenges and successes. They would set an action plan for the following 30 days, implementing concepts they were learning. At the following meeting, they reported back on how they did—what worked, what didn't, and what they learned in the process.

The most difficult part of this program was marketing it. As I networked with people, I shared with them what I had created, what members would gain from it, and the types of people who might be interested in joining.

I saw a lot of head-nodding, understanding what I had created and why, but only a light smattering of interest or referrals.

I was frustrated at myself for not being able to generate more members. I considered shutting down the program before it even really got going.

Then I met Ron.

In his late sixties, Ron had been an independent consultant (executive coaching, board coaching, and leadership development) for thirty years. I was so impressed with Ron's success and even more so with his staying power. During our first meeting, I peppered him with questions about his business and experiences.

As we learned each other's background, I shared that I was an introvert, and the difficulty I had experienced being out on my own. He laughed and admitted that he was too.

That surprised me, but I must admit that in that moment I felt known. Not just because of the introvert connection but also because of the shared experience of trying to build an indie consulting business as an introvert, which means relying on yourself for business development and income.

We talked about my interim CIO business and then I mentioned my struggling leadership development program. I described what I was trying to build and the types of individuals who might be interested in joining.

Ron pulled out his cell phone and started calling people.

Right then and there. In the coffee shop. No hesitation.

"Hi, Jane? It's Ron. I'm sitting here across from my new friend,

John Hughes. He's looking for up-and-coming technology leaders to join his leadership development program. I thought you might have some people in your IT organization who would be interested. Oh, great! I'll get the two of you connected and let you take it from there."

He called three people, one after the other. Same conversation.

I just sat there. I had never experienced anything like that. I felt uncomfortable. Very humbled. And yet honored. Ron barely knew me, but there he was extending his good name and trust to me! Throughout each call, Ron would look at me as if he'd known and trusted me his whole life.

Ron not only helped me and my leadership development program, he single-handedly resurrected it. Several people joined as a direct result of those three phone calls.

In addition to that help, he gave me another gift that day. He showed me what it was like to feel known and trusted. Both are powerful gifts that we can choose to give to people in our lives, business or personal.

Ron continues to stay top of mind for me (and for many others in his network), not because of the superb executive coaching work he provides his clients, but because of who he is and how he makes others feel.

Several years after that coffee shop experience, Ron and I still actively share referrals and introduce people to each other. He truly created a legacy for himself by what he teaches others through his genuineness and generosity.

Oh, and Ron is living the life he desired. Woven in between consulting engagements, he travels the world a few times each year, fly-fishing with his wife.

That is how it's done. How helping and giving of oneself creates long-lasting business success, long-lasting friendships, and an abundant life.

A generous person will prosper; whoever
refreshes others will be refreshed.

Proverbs 11:25

A helping hand

Genuinely offering my time and resources for free to help people inside and outside of my network is an investment in them, in my network, and in myself. I have always been happy to make these investments, without expectation of anything in return.

Any expectation of return creates resentment when your expectations aren't realized (which will happen way too often), and the resentment will drag you down and hold you back. You'll be tossing some heavy-duty monkey wrenches into your indie engine.

There are unlimited ways to help people. Every person in your network has a need, likely multiple needs. We keep most of our needs hidden from others, especially within professional circles. It takes time and trust to get beyond the surface to where the deepest needs are hidden, far from superficial networking discussions.

Following your passions

The book you're holding is an outcome of helping other independent consultants. Indies always have a desire to learn better strategies for developing business, and I'm happy to be an open book for them. I love the conversations and have them several times a month. My passion for this topic of business development and for helping others is a reason I continue to receive introductions to people seeking these insights. And those introductions lead to even more introductions, *and* to additional opportunities to help and give.

This is who I am, and it works extremely well for me. What's your passion? How can you use it to help and invest in others?

Passions are contagious. When we do things that we love, we're energized, and it shows. We look engaged and excited, because we are. When we learn or experience new things in an upbeat, positive way, from an upbeat, positive person, we want to share that experience and passion with others.

When I meet with one of these passionate people, I'm already listing in my head the people that I want to introduce to them. I want others to experience what I just experienced.

Follow your passions. Give away those things that excite and energize you. You will excite and energize others in the process and make yourself contagious. Along the way, your network will grow, your business will grow, and you will grow.

Investing in others

I get pure joy out of helping people grow as leaders. I used to push this on those in whom I saw talent (yes, quite obnoxious), but now I wait for them to pursue it. It's much better to desire and pursue growth than to have it thrust on you.

Most people in my network know that they can reach out to me and schedule a coffee for a leadership discussion. I do this for them, and for the internal reward that I receive.

Nicole worked for me a few years ago in IT with one of my clients. I recognized her talent for leadership, but it was fairly raw. (Even she admitted this.) We worked one-on-one for a few weeks to draw out her leadership strengths. She was tactical in her approach to work, which is appropriate for a technical resource. But I wanted to draw out the more visionary, strategic, and enterprise mindset that I saw within her. Eventually, she pushed back and said she wasn't ready. I understood and let it go.

About a year later, she called me and asked if the offer was still good. "Yes, of course!" I said.

Since that phone call, and over the next couple of years, we met every three or four months for coffee. In this time, she moved into a technical lead role at a new company, was promoted to director, and is now being pursued by other companies for broader leadership roles.

I truly love watching people grow and expand beyond what they thought possible. In those moments, I feel fulfilled.

Do you have a talent that propels others forward that you love to give away? Invest it in your network.

Making life easier for other indies

Another way to help and give to your network is by making life easier for other indies. I often share agreements (and other templates and documents) with those in my network. I've developed some decent agreements over the years, which have been reviewed and improved upon by clients and their legal counsel. We all need solid agreements that protect our business as well as protect our clients. These documents help make life a little easier for other indies.

Aside from referrals, agreements are a valuable asset for any indie, especially for those who are just starting out. Getting proven agreements from other consultants allows them to avoid having an attorney draft an agreement for each new type of engagement, saving them quite a bit of time and a lot of money.

Mine are written in plain English (versus Latin and legalese). However, I didn't start from a blank slate myself. My friend, Larry, an indie sales and marketing consultant, developed a one-page agreement years ago for his clients. He was proud that it was written in plain ole English. I asked for a copy, and he happily shared it.

That one-pager has sprouted several different agreements, which I've shared with others, and which have likely sprouted dozens more.

What tangible items have you developed that you could share in order to make business life easier for others in your network? These could be agreements, statements of work, tools (spreadsheets are a great example), templates, forms, formulas, etc.

The gift of helping and giving

There's such a deep fulfillment and satisfaction that can only come from giving of who we are. In serving others, we also serve our God, and this pleases Him. By being part of a giving network of people, I have been richly rewarded by all things non-monetary.

If you genuinely help and serve others—giving of your time, talents, and all—people will remember you, introduce you to people in their networks, create opportunities for you, and refer business to you. They don't do these things because of what you do as a consultant, but because of who you are, how you make others feel, and how you treat others.

Helping and giving have been vitally core to my business development engine and have enabled me to create income without selling.

The education business

When I first launched as an independent consultant, I knew I was in the education business. I wasn't certain that everyone would know what an interim CIO was (or any of my other myriad services) or the value in hiring one. So, it was my job to educate them.

This put me in the education business.

Initially, I educated via my website and some marketing collateral that a firm had created for me. This didn't get me very far since few people were visiting my website or reading my fliers.

I wasn't seeing any incoming calls or opportunities.

The marketing material didn't make a lick of difference for me. That is, until I began to network and build relationships with real human beings. Marketing is too impersonal, too separated from the buyer, to do much good, especially for us indies.

Getting into the education game

Through my one-on-one networking meetings, I began to see the connection between helping and educating (and doing these consistently). They are a powerful combination for any indie consultant, especially for those of us who don't want to sell or be viewed as a salesperson.

My drumbeat was an important component of how I educated others about my business. It was quick, concise, and memorable. It proved very effective at networking events, where you don't always get a lot of time with other attendees. A quick and easy drumbeat also allowed me to focus more on the other person, so it proved doubly effective.

In order to further enhance my education effort, and if time allowed, I would share a success story. I aimed to get through a story in just a minute or so. This meant boiling down a six-month engagement into only the meaningful highlights.

It would go something like this:

"I finished an interim CIO engagement recently with Cantril Corp. Jenny, an independent consultant herself, introduced me to their CFO. She had been consulting with them and thought I might be able to help with their IT situation. They were looking for greater strategic results out of IT and needed the team to better understand and meet the operational needs of the business. They also had a software project that was going sideways. I was their interim CIO for about six months. We implemented a way to prioritize strategic projects based on business value, realigned the IT team to better listen to and meet the operational needs of the business, and got the software project back on track for success. IT is now more engaged with the business and they've made a difference on the top line and the bottom line. And we did this without any people changes, which was my favorite part. The same team that frustrated the business before is now being cheered on by them."

I always tried to reference client names and brands that people would recognize. You earn greater credibility when you reference well-known brands as clients, even if they're only locally known.

The highlights that I tried to hit on in a brief "educational" moment were: (1) the client name, (2) who introduced me to them, (3) the client's situation, (4) the key improvements I focused on, and (5) the state in which I left the client.

The key was not for the listener to repeat any of the story. The key was to give enough information to help others understand the value of an interim CIO, but not so much that I bogged them down in detail to the point of being forgettable. When someone in your network tells a buyer that you can make a difference in a difficult situation (even without the detail), they just completed 50 percent of the sale for you.

Referrals are powerful. They're what you're after. *Helping and educating throughout your networking efforts will be the seeds of your referrals... and the seeds of your success.*

Referrals will show up. Just be your genuine, giving self—with a touch of educator thrown in.

You plant, He takes care of the rest

Ron changed my business mindset and gave me greater hope for success. Through his example, he gave me confidence that an introverted entrepreneur could survive on their own, and he set an example for how helping and educating can be the seeds of indie success. It's worked for him for thirty years, and now fourteen years for me. It can work for you too.

Relentlessly sow the seeds of helping and educating with everyone you meet, across the fertile fields of your network. Nurture your fields by staying in touch with your network, helping and educating wherever you can. Be consistent and persistent and your business will grow. Heck, *you* will grow.

Do not worry about when the seeds will germinate and bloom. That is in God's hands, not yours. Put your faith in Him, that He will bring the fruit forward in its own time. As a faith-filled business owner, focus on what is in your control—planting and nurturing the seeds of helping, giving, and educating. Not only are these in your control, they are more fun and rewarding to focus on than trying to force seeds to germinate and bloom before they're ready.

No selling. No sales process to follow. No chasing leads. You simply get to be your awesome, genuine, giving self.

CHAPTER 5

Questions for Guidance and Action

1. What are you passionate about that you could use to serve others in your network?

2. What talents do you have that you could use to invest in others in your network?

3. What business tools have you developed that you would happily share with others to make life easier for them?

4. In addition to your drumbeat, what stories or examples will you use to educate others about your business?

5. What is the single biggest action you will take today to move yourself closer to a client engagement?

6. What is the next single biggest action you will take?

7. And the next?

UNSELLING NOTES

"And if that doesn't work, we'll print up some t-shirts, fly a banner over the stadium at half-time, and paint your logo on your car."

Marketing and Other Games of Chance

Lazy hands make for poverty, but diligent hands bring wealth.

Proverbs 10:4

~ Key Point ~

As an indie consultant, marketing won't bring you business, only people will.

Welcome to Vegas, baby!

I've been to Las Vegas many times, mostly on business. Throughout those twenty or so trips, I've only lost money gambling once. I'm certain of this, because I've only gambled once—on my first trip—when I lost it all.

Never again.

As a small-town Ohio boy, I was definitely overwhelmed stepping into a casino for the first time. I would have loved to try blackjack, but I didn't want to sit with skilled players and show them how much I didn't know. (A bit too embarrassing of a scenario for me.) I walked around for a few minutes scanning the different games, all the while going into sensory overload with the lights glaring, music blaring, machines pinging and dinging, voices and conversations intermingling into one loud hum, and cigarette smoke crawling all over my body.

The lure of the slots pulled me in, though, and I decided to endure the overload.

I dropped coin after coin into the first machine. I looked for patterns. I watched other players at machines near mine, and looked for patterns there too. I moved machines and started again. I must have deciphered a pattern, because within thirty minutes, I was up 50 percent!

What do you do when you're up in Vegas? Play more, of course!

So, I stuck with the pattern. But something changed, and I didn't see it soon enough. I lost it all. I gave my winnings back, and my original investment. *That's $20 I'll never see again!*

That was my limit, and I stuck to it. My gambling career ended within the same hour it had started. I have no regrets. I knew the odds and I like my money. The two really don't mix very well.

Your odds are not good, either

Your odds in Vegas are not good. Whether playing the slots, cards, wheels, or even dice in a back alley. That's a given. It's all a crap shoot.

Marketing for indie consultants can feel like an even bigger gamble. I know. I've lost a lot of money gambling on marketing. Way more than $20.

Never again.

Larger companies have marketing budgets that allow them to test different strategies, take losses, learn, and continually improve their results. We indies don't have that luxury (with time or money). We need to be right the first time, and pretty much every time.

While I am a huge fan of marketing, marketing is not a huge fan of indies. It's cruel, in fact. Marketing will steal your time, take your money, and leave you feeling taken advantage of.

It's kind of like running full speed into a brick wall that you didn't even see. Except you did see it. You just didn't want to believe it was there.

We want marketing to work for us because we want to take the quick and easy route to income. As consumers, we're inundated with marketing. We see how much is out there, so it must work, right? But, for indies it doesn't work.

I get it. I desperately wanted it to work as badly as you do. But, it's just not a reality for independent consultants.

Over a dozen years now into my own indie business, I still have a bad taste in my mouth from the thousands and thousands of dollars I spent on marketing and marketing-related materials in my first couple of years. Way over $10,000. And I had very little income at the time, so I took this money out of savings.

Ouch!

I truly believed that if I had all of the makings of a professional business—designed and built by a marketing firm—clients would be calling two seconds after the website went live and the fliers hit the streets. That dream turned nightmare.

I hired a firm, on retainer no less. (Retainer simply means that I guaranteed, in writing, their income… and my loss.) They built for me a very professional website, logo, marketing fliers, a PowerPoint template with my fancy new logo and colors, business cards, white papers, and who knows what other bells and whistles and upgrades I opted for.

None of these brought me business. None of them. Not even the website.

You know that sinking feeling in your gut that hits you when you drive a brand new car off the lot and you think, "I just paid $50,000 for this?! I liked my old car—rust, dents, and all. I was happy and comfortable with it. What was I thinking?!"

Yep. That's the feeling that hit me after I drove that website off the lot.

Marketing for indies is like throwing spaghetti (sauce included) up against a wall hoping something will stick. Anything.

It doesn't. Nothing sticks. It just slides down the wall creating a mess that only you can clean up.

Yes, this is what we indies do. We waste time and money throwing spaghetti at walls instead of investing time in people, people who can actually hire us and refer business to us.

Marketing can definitely reach people outside your network by spreading your message to an audience that you can't see and that doesn't yet see you. And, yes, this is awesome and valuable and brings great hope. The problem is, marketing is an expensive and risky venture, *especially for indies!* We don't have the time or money it takes to get it right.

There are just too many choices in strategy, in technique, and in marketing firms. One key component of marketing involves trial and error—try something, learn, make adjustments, try again. This costs time and money! And every firm you speak with—whether a single-shingle or a global firm—all have their perspective of what works and what doesn't. And they will strive to put you in *their* box because they know their box really well, they have expertise in it, and they're efficient at executing it. But their box may not be the box you need!

Before you hire a marketing firm, you need to understand your business. Thoroughly. So thoroughly that when you see a marketing strategy, you know immediately whether or not it will work for you.

Do not put your hope and trust in a marketing strategy, or in a marketing firm. It will not pay off.

Marketing and marketing collateral *will not* bring you business. Only people will. People who know you, know what you do, and trust you.

People talk, paper walks

I've seen tons of marketing pieces (including single-page fliers) from independent consultants over the years—enough to shred and hold a ticker-tape parade for the marketing firms that created them. Some are written quite well and of high quality; others are wordy, confusing, and of low quality. But, as marketing pieces, none of them were effective. They just don't bring in business. They bring higher costs, lower bank accounts, and dashed hopes, and they keep us from doing the real work necessary to bring dollars in the door.

There are three primary reasons that one-page marketing pieces, and most marketing for that matter, don't work for independent consultants.

First, most indies don't understand their message well enough to ensure it is clear, succinct, and resonates with prospects and referral partners. So, they write wordy fliers and wordy websites, hoping that something will speak to the reader.

But this puts the burden on the reader. You're asking them to pull out the exact right value proposition that matches their need. That's your responsibility, not theirs. Besides, nobody wants more work. And it kind of goes against any indie consultant's core purpose, which is to make life easier for our clients. If your flier—or website—makes them work, they're likely already saying "No!"

You would be better off just using a full-page image or picture on the flier, no words, and your logo in the bottom right. After all, a picture is worth a thousand words. In two seconds, your prospect would get it, and they would know that you get it too. You're way closer to a yes using a picture worth a thousand words, than typing a thousand words and hoping they see the right picture.

Second, most indie marketing pieces don't work because they're not professionally designed. (Sometimes we hire firms, and sometimes we hire ourselves.) PowerPoint, Word, Adobe Illustrator, Keynote, and other software tools used for creating marketing materials are powerful. So is an M1 Abrams battle tank. It just needs to be in capable hands.

So, ignore that notion you have about saving money by creating your own marketing materials (including logos, websites, fliers, and anything else requiring a professional designer). Even if you happen to be a design expert, hire someone else. You're too close to the project. At the very least, get a second opinion before you operate on yourself.

Graphics, colors, spacing, balance, flow, even white space all matter. You and I don't want our clients going with a low-quality solution for the services that we offer. We would prefer they hire us. Do the same. Practice what you preach. If you desperately want marketing collateral, hire a professional to design and create all things marketing for you.

If you hand out low-quality marketing pieces, you will be shouting loudly and clearly to everyone, "This is the quality I put into my work, so if you're looking for this level of quality, hire me!"

They won't.

And, third, indie marketing materials miss the mark due to lack of consistent branding.

That fancy new flier you just printed on your home printer doesn't match the look and feel and message of your website, which doesn't match your newsletter, which doesn't match your business cards, which don't match the pens stamped with your logo (all two thousand of them sitting in a box in the garage).

Inconsistent branding communicates that you've not really put much thought into your brand.

Think about where you shop for your clothes, or the car you drive. Consciously, or subconsciously, you are identifying with those *brands*. They have a *message*, and a *look*, and a *feel* that appeal to you.

In 2003, I bought a new Honda Pilot. At the time, I definitely identified with the look and feel of that car—reliable, safe, affordable, a touch of rugged, and enough room for the whole family, plus the dog and soccer gear. That was me in 2003. In 2016, I finally bought another new car. You can be sure it wasn't a Pilot. The kids are all out of the house, no more soccer gear, and even the dog has moved on. The new car is small, sleek, sporty, elegant, not so affordable, and not so safe at the speeds I drive (just kidding!). It's like the automaker designed that car and all of its look and feel just for me. Which, in many ways, they did.

That's what you want with your branding. Put yourself in your buyer's shoes. What look and feel are your buyers expecting? Safe? Trusted? Professional? Expert? Playful? Reliable? Rugged? Edgy?

Your brand isn't defined by just words. It includes look (colors, images, shapes, fonts, layout), and feel (quality, emotions, texture, movement, identity), *and their consistency across all of your business.*

Branding is one place where you need to draw lines of what is acceptable and what isn't, and then color inside the lines. Color outside too much, and you will confuse people. You will especially confuse your buyer, but also your referral partners—they won't have the confidence to recommend you or refer business to you.

Make it easy for your buyer by defining your brand and being consistent with it. Give them all of the confidence in the world that you know who you are, what you stand for, and what they can expect from you.

My own painful reality

Looking back on the first couple of years of my indie business, I can honestly say that I used marketing as an excuse to not be out networking. I hid behind my marketing materials.

I wanted my website and fliers and white papers out in public doing the work that I didn't want to do. But I learned the hard and very expensive way that only I can create business.

That was my painful reality. I don't want it to become yours.

So, as indies, we need to be very careful with our marketing strategies and marketing spend. The time and dollars invested in anything marketing related has very little chance of producing results. Very little. No piece of paper, website, book, newsletter, webinar, logo shirt, YouTube channel, or airplane banner will bring you clients.

Hiding behind marketing won't build your business.

You need to get out and talk to people. Network. Help. Educate.

Nothing can take the place of you. Nothing. Marketing is of no value until you build out your network.

Only when you have a trusted network in place—hundreds of people who know you, understand what you do, and trust you—will you be able to use marketing to *amplify* and *expand* your message. At that point, you'll have a solid and trusted network upon which your marketing can ride.

Your path to indie business success isn't through marketing, it's through people—people you are personally connected with—people whom *you know*, and who *know you*.

Where marketing money *can* help you

In the beginning

In the beginning, John wasted a lot of time and money on marketing. He should have been out meeting every Adam and Eve he could find, so he could beget business a lot sooner than he actually did.

Revelation 1

> *The dragon stood on the shore of the sea. And I*
> *saw a beast coming out of the sea. It had ten horns*
> *and seven heads, with ten crowns on its horns,*
> *and on each head a blasphemous name.*

Revelation 13:1

As an indie consultant, I would not be surprised if one of those names was marketing!

Please, don't get me wrong. I actually love marketing. Just not for indie consultants in the genesis of their business. You need to get to the book of Acts before marketing will be of value, where the fire is lit and the word spreads rapidly and organically from person to person.

Revelation 2

After crashing and burning—trying to use marketing to develop business—here is what I learned are the marketing basics* for any indie consultant:

  ✓ Business name
  ✓ Logo

---

* *These are the marketing basics, not the financial or legal basics. Consult with a CPA and attorney prior to starting any business.*

✓   Website
✓   Email address
✓   Business cards
✓   A punch card (or app) from your favorite café

Anything more in the beginning and you will be wasting your time and money.

Each of these items, individually and together, give an indie instant credibility and believability… *if they're created with quality and consistent branding.*

(OK, maybe the punch card isn't so critical, but if you are consistently out networking, having a loyalty card from a local café will bring you quite a few free sips.)

Add these items to the ongoing networking, helping, and educating we've already discussed, along with superior client service delivery, and you have a solid success model for an indie consulting business.

Prime this pump unceasingly. If you can keep this up without your arm getting tired, you will soon find yourself in the enviable position of unselling.

Let's go a little deeper into these basic marketing needs.

Business name

The most difficult part of selecting a business name is finding one where the domain name (.com, .net, .co, etc.) is still available. It's a frustrating process. I've done it several times and it's never easy, especially if you just want to use your personal name. The first several domain names you'll try will have already been taken. Stick with your search, though, and be prepared to get a little creative.

If you know for a fact that you will be the only person in your business, consider using your name—first and last name, or just last name, or just first name. I don't recommend using initials. You want to be remembered, so unless you're IBM, AT&T, Mr. T, or Jay Z, I suggest steering clear of initials in your business name. You want it to be memorable and brandable.

What matters most is the way it sounds—the feeling and message it conveys and how credible and memorable it is.

Brainstorm a broad set of options; put them in front of family, friends, and strangers; and ask them, "Which company would you hire as a consulting firm?" Even if they don't know what the firm does, they'll still be able to tell you which they trust, or which they most identify with.

I recommend seeking out an independent branding expert who has experience naming companies and creating brands and logos. Speak to several experts and select the one you're most comfortable with. You will pay them for a few hours of work, but it will be more than worth the investment.

Once you pick a name, be sure to "Google" it, "Bing" it, or "DuckDuckGo" it to see what pops up. You don't want to tread on any existing service marks or trademarks, nor do you want to compete with lots of similar names.

Logo

A high-quality logo will grant you instant credibility, believability, and professionalism, and will lay the foundation for brand building.

I highly recommend working with a professional designer. There are also online resources where you can have professional options created without spending a lot of money.

Know your buyer and have them in mind when you design your logo. What would appeal to them or resonate with them? My buyers are typically C-level executives, so I went with a very professional look and feel. Your buyers need to identify with your logo as well.

Like business names, logos can be trademarked, so be sure yours doesn't infringe on an existing logo.

Website

You do need a website. It will give you a great deal of credibility. Don't expect to get business from it, though. With good search engine optimization (SEO), you may get some business, but as an independent consultant don't expect it or rely on it.

Even with every aspect of our lives going mobile and the ongoing rise of apps, having a website is still a must. With website platforms like SquareSpace, however, you can build a site and have it automatically render as a mobile app as well. This will save you a boatload of time and money. Very cool.

And there's no need to go big with volumes of content. Keep it simple. Save your nickels. It's not so much about the amount of content, anyway. Your website is nothing more than a credibility check. When someone hears about you, they will go to your website to see if you're real, if you might be someone they would want to work with, and if your services match their needs. They will spend only a minute or two there, not much more.

As with everything else, your website message needs to be clear, concise, and consistent. You want the site's content, look, and feel to give your buyers confidence that you're serious about your business, that you are a professional and know what you're doing, and that you understand and can confidently solve their problem.

Email address

Yes, some people still use email, so, until some junior high kid in their room releases an app for telepathic communication, it will be important for you to have an email address.

Ideally, you will use the format *yourname@yourwebsite.com*.

Please try not to use @gmail or @outlook or @anything except your website domain name. I do know successful indies who use a generic email provider (e.g., Gmail), but you will gain greater credibility and believability with an email address based on your website domain name.

Business cards

Business cards are still the expected leave-behind at networking meetings and events. Yes, they typically end up in a drawer with hundreds of their cardboard cousins, or in file 13. But don't leave home without them!

If your logo is professional, and your cards are of high quality, you will be communicating that you are serious about your business. You are establishing trust with your network and increasing your chances of receiving referrals from everyone who receives one of your quality cards.

After all, it's not just a business card, it represents the quality of your brand and services—the quality of *you*.

While we're on this topic, please don't be a CEO, president, or business owner; at least, don't put these titles on your business card. You will lose credibility. Be almost anything else. Be a Consultant, Sr. Consultant, Principal, Project Manager, Architect, Executive Coach, Advisor, or even Chief Bottle Washer or Janitor to the Stars (at least these are funny and memorable and invite fun dialogue).

It's just not credible to be the CEO or president of your own indie business. Your clients aren't hiring a CEO or president. You can be one on your incorporation papers and in your head, but not on your business card.

If you treat your business name, logo, website, email address, and business cards professionally and with respect, then you are telling others that you will treat them with respect as well, especially your clients.

The irony of indie marketing

Marketing won't bring you business, only people who know you, trust you, and remember you will.

Marketing can, however, be the oxygen that you blow on the fire of your *already active and effective network*. It's not the thing that jumpstarts your business in the beginning, or when you're seeking a new client. If you've built a powerful and trusted network, it will provide enough referrals to keep you busy—so busy that you may not even need to invest in marketing at all. So, ironically, marketing will work for an indie right about the time they don't need it.

CHAPTER 6

Questions for Guidance and Action

1. What will your business name be?

2. Will you have a logo? Who will design it?

3. Will you have a website? Who will design it, write it, build it, maintain it?

4. Will you have business cards? Who will design them? What will your title be?

5. What other marketing material will you start with? Why will you need this?

6. Have you consulted with an attorney and a CPA?

7. What is the single biggest action you will take today to move yourself closer to a client engagement?

8. What is the next single biggest action you will take?

9. And the next?

UNSELLING NOTES

"Umm, okay, so, let's continue reading on slide #136..."

Writing and Speaking

For the mouth speaks what the heart is full of.

Luke 6:45

~ *Key Point* ~

Writing and speaking can propel your indie business, if you can be entertaining.

The master of entertainment

Patrick Lencioni is a master, maybe *the* master, of using writing and speaking to develop consulting business. The *Wall Street Journal* recently named him one of the top five speakers in the nation. He's also sold over five million books. His consulting firm, The Table Group, is in high demand as a direct result of his writing and speaking talents.

Lencioni is a rare breed. His books are written in fable format, engaging his readers from start to finish. He tells entertaining stories, in person or in pen. He comes alive on stage just as his storytelling comes alive in his books. He excels at both mediums equally well, and both pull business into his consulting firm.

His model works because his stories *amaze*. He combines insightful, transformative content with entertainment. One without the other wouldn't work. In a word, his work is compelling.

Do you want to be like Lencioni?

It's an important question. Think about this for a moment. Do you chase only what will bring in business? Or do you chase what you truly love and enjoy?

Many people chase the money. But, if you don't love and enjoy what you do, it will show, and will bring limited success and frustration.

If you want to leverage speaking and writing as an avenue for business development, you will need to have the insightful and transformative content that business leaders are hungry for, and you'll need to deliver it in an entertaining fashion.

I would rather entertain and hope that people learned something than educate people and hope they were entertained.

Walt Disney

Amen! That's no Mickey Mouse statement! If you take one thing away from this chapter, it's this quote from Disney.

You are better off entertaining your audience and interspersing your wisdom throughout, versus formulating a speech or presentation filled to the brim with your wisdom yet miss engaging them.

Entertainment in a presentation or speech doesn't have to be humorous, though it most often is. Humans love to laugh. Doing so releases endorphins and puts us in a better mood and state of mind for learning. We feel better after a good laugh, and as a speaker or writer, you'll always be remembered for making your audience laugh.

I didn't understand the need to entertain when I first started speaking. I assumed everyone wanted insight, information, and knowledge. That they wanted to be taught the things I knew and learn from my experiences. And the more I could cram into the hour, the better.

So, I stripped my speeches down to their raw nakedness: Information. Facts. Lessons learned. Processes. The stories and characters and settings that brought these about? Minor details. Superfluous. Unnecessary.

I grabbed my high-powered firehose, opened it up, and drowned my audience in information. Force-fed from a firehose. No stories. No humor. No rip-roaring yarns. Just fact after fact after fact from an industrial-strength hose.

I was after *quantity*. They wanted *quality*. They already had enough on their minds, enough weighing on them with their job responsibilities and personal lives. They didn't need me adding to that burden. They don't want you adding to it either. They want a break. A respite. They need to lighten the load a bit before more gets piled on. They want to be *entertained*.

Don't overwhelm them with information or underwhelm them with a boring style. Be like Mr. Disney and give 'em what they want—a little insight and education wrapped up in an entertaining speech or presentation.

Speaking tips

I'm not a naturally gifted speaker. I'm more of a sharer of information—a teacher. I never developed the knack for entertaining or verbal storytelling. This means that I need to lean on my writing and networking abilities more than my speaking talents. This is who I am and I'm OK with that.

Know who you are. What you're naturally good at. What you love.

Do that.

If you continue to do it exceptionally well over a long period of time (*years*, not just weeks or months), you'll find more and more people following you and wanting to be connected with you. This brings more opportunities to help and educate others, which will flow into more consulting work.

Whether you're a natural at speaking or a nervous Nellie, you will be more effective if you put the audience first, by giving them what they want—insight, knowledge, and information presented in an entertaining fashion. This is how you can leverage speaking to propel your indie business to its highest heights.

You don't need to sing, juggle, do magic tricks, or tap dance to be entertaining. You do need to tell stories and use real-life examples that draw your audiences into your world, so they can see, hear, smell, feel, and taste what you're describing. Then they'll be able to relate to your content and relate to *you*. This makes your content, and you, stick—it makes you memorable.

You can also tell anecdotes from your career to make your points come to life. Anecdotes—short, amusing, or interesting stories about a real incident or person—give your audience another way to understand, relate to, and remember an important point.

Here's one of my favorite examples I've used when talking about the power of trust:

I was new in a CIO role many years ago. One of my managers came to me and asked if he could go talk with our senior vice president of marketing. I gave him an odd look and asked why he needed permission to talk with someone else in the company.

"Because we always needed permission before. I'm just doing what I was asked to do."

"OK, here's the deal, Dan. I trust you. You don't need to ask me for permission to speak with anyone inside the company, or outside, for that matter. You're good at what you do. You know what I expect of you, so, please, just go make that happen."

I didn't see Dan for two years!

OK, two years might be a bit exaggerated, but not much. The point is, we all experience even simple moments like this in our careers and even daily work life. It's a matter of being on the lookout for them; remembering them; and presenting them in a relatable, teachable, and entertaining way.

Telling personal or family stories to a business audience also bring valuable points to life. And they make you *human*—vulnerable, relatable, real. This works beautifully, because humans tend to want to hire other humans.

Here's a simple example I've used about persistence:

When my three kids were younger, ages ranging from nine to fourteen, they desperately wanted a dog. They promised they would be happier kids, do their chores without complaining, get better grades, and that the sun and stars would most certainly shine brighter. I couldn't get past the downside of a pet bigger than a hamster, and said no. They tried multiple approaches, including begging, pouty faces, and promises that I would never have to do anything to take care of it. Nothing worked for them. I continued to hold the line and say no. (I just saw a dog as more work for me.) Then my daughter somehow came up with the idea that they could get my attention, and approval, if they approached the problem using my language. At twelve years old, she put together a business case for a dog! She even got executive approval—signatures from her mom and every other parent on our block! I was presented with a business case that I couldn't turn down. My

kids' desire, creativity, and persistence needed to be rewarded.
Sophie, a very playful Jack-a-poo, joined our family soon
after, and I spent the next several years cleaning up after her.
(And thoroughly enjoying her.)

A bit of cuteness and humor plays well with an audience. But, you can also be dramatic.

Col. Anthony Wood, United States Marine Corps (Ret.), gave one of the best speeches I've ever heard. To tell you the truth, I don't remember laughing a single time during his talk. The topic just didn't call for humor—the dramatic extraction of Americans and Vietnamese during the Fall of Saigon in April 1975. An hour of edge-of-your-seat drama, uplifting at times, heartbreaking at others. The leadership lessons and images he painted have stayed with me for years.

Take your audience on a journey *with* you instead of giving them the facts you collected from your journey. Help them feel as though they're a part of the action. This is memorable. This is entertaining!

We'd rather be dead

Jerry Seinfeld, in his monologue for the Season 4 *Seinfeld* episode, "The Pilot," shared the curious fact that people have ranked fear of public speaking higher than fear of death. "This means to the average person," he quips, "that if you have to go to a funeral, you're better off in the casket than doing the eulogy."

If you'd rather be dead than speak in front of a group of people, there's hope for you. Public speaking can still be part of your indie engine.

Here's how.

Sitting on panels

If you're asked to speak at an event, let the organizers know that instead of standing onstage all by your lonesome, you would welcome the opportunity to sit on a panel.

With panels, you don't have to prepare a speech or presentation. You just show up and contribute your insights, expertise, and sense of humor. You also get to rely on the grace of the other panelists, as well as the moderator. The best part? *The pressure's not all on you!* Compare that with speaking solo, where it's your sole responsibility to keep the audience interested and engaged for an hour, with all of those eyeballs bearing down on you, waiting for you to wow them with wisdom.

Panels are way more fun than solo speaking gigs—especially if they're structured as an open forum, allowing for questions and witty banter between panelists.

Moderating panels

Moderating panels can be fun too. There's more prep work as the moderator than just sitting on the panel, but it's a great way to be onstage and gain exposure without the pressure of being there alone. You get to ask the questions and guide the conversation, as well as sneak in a comment or two yourself.

The key to panels? It's no different than with speaking or writing—be insightful, be informative, be engaging, and be entertaining.

Leading roundtables

For smaller groups, two to fifteen people, roundtables are another way to lighten the stress and worry of speeches. You get to simply sit at the table and facilitate a discussion. Everyone learns from everyone else, so you're not always on the spot. Attendees get to ask questions, contribute ideas and insights, and tell their own stories.

Because of the intimate setting, this is also the best scenario for developing relationships.

OK, we've talked enough about talking. Let's move on to the wonderful world of words.

Writing—Books

If you're at all like me—if you've ever felt insecure or inadequate when it comes to public speaking—then writing might be the ticket for you.

My first book, *Haunting the CEO*, was written in fable format. It's entertaining. I've had many people tell me they read it in a single sitting. Even non-business people have read it and enjoyed it. It's not the best thing ever written, but it does hook the reader and pull them through a story, while sharing some leadership principles along the way. People appreciate the story format. It works well for Patrick Lencioni, and it worked well for me.

I discovered the story format quite by accident. To be honest, it was more like I tripped over it. I was reading Lencioni's *The Five Dysfunctions of a Team*, and about halfway through it I said to myself, "I can do this!"

I immediately sat down and began writing. No story. No characters. No outline. No plan. Just the leadership principles that I wanted to share with others.

The story, or fable format, resonated with me. It seemed natural. It truly felt like the book was writing itself. Where I struggled to use stories in my speeches, I succeeded at using them in writing.

Haunting the CEO definitely brought me business. At first, it brought only speaking engagements. But, as the book spread among the business community, it led to introductions to C-level executives, which led to client work. The book became a valuable part of my indie business engine. It worked well for four primary reasons:

1. It was short and easy to read

2. It had lots of good leadership principles that readers could understand and apply

3. It was entertaining (a little dramatic, some humor, engaging dialogue)

4. It was relatable (multiple characters, someone for everyone to relate to)

It also worked because I found an easy and natural way to write. That experience taught me that I love writing dialogue and creating stories and characters.

How do you find what is natural for you? Read different authors and styles, both fiction and nonfiction. Read about writing. But most of all, write! Don't be afraid to try and fail. Focus on identifying what feels right, and what doesn't. Seek to learn what is most natural and comfortable for you. Then seek to continually improve.

But most of all, write. A lot. And edit your writing. A lot. And when you're done writing and editing, write and edit some more.

Not interested in writing books? That's OK! There are many other awesome avenues for you to leverage your writing for business development.

Writing—Articles and Blogs

Most business media outlets (print and online) are always on the lookout for great content. If you can write and have something new, unique, or insightful to say, seek to be a guest columnist for print and online outlets in your area. You're not after paid gigs; you're simply after broader exposure for your business and your services.

And what about blogging? Regular blogging will build your name and brand recognition, especially if you're already viewed as a thought leader in your industry. Post blogs on your website and on LinkedIn, or on other appropriate social media sites.

If you do get an article published, be sure to let your network know about it via your website, LinkedIn, Twitter, and other social media sites.

Writing—Newsletters

For a couple of years, before I wrote my first book, I produced an email newsletter as part of my business.

My number one goal was to just get my name in peoples' inbox. If they opened my newsletter, I wanted them to be greeted with something that entertained them. It didn't matter so much what I wrote, as long as it was entertaining and related to my business of interim CIO and IT leadership.

The newsletter worked well. I received lots of compliments. I should have kept it going, but I got too busy. That consistency would have paid dividends. Looking back, I wish I'd hired someone to produce and manage the newsletter for me so that it didn't stop.

Email-based newsletters are still a good way to remind people that you exist, while also reminding them of the value you deliver. Keep them simple. Make them visually appealing. Don't cram them full of words and pictures and links. Instead, include lots of white space for the reader to take a visual and mental break.

Newsletters help you stay top of mind. That's what you're after. The fact that you provide great and amazing content is simply icing on the cake.

How to be a good writer when you're not

Let's say you're not a great writer—or even a good one—but want to leverage writing for your business.

Great news! There's hope for you.

You don't need to be perfect with grammar and punctuation. Readability is more important.

Your writing just needs to be *clear* (a single main point and no rambling), *concise* (as few words as possible), and contain a *logical flow* from top to bottom.

Don't bang out something in ten minutes and post it. Write a draft, and then edit it several times, clarifying your main point and stripping out unnecessary words along the way.

If you always find yourself staring at a blank page, here's a suggestion for you.

Baby steps.

Break down that 1,000-word blog you want to write, or article, or the first draft of that book chapter into something smaller. Something manageable. Something you can achieve.

To get to that first draft, brainstorm the top ten points you want to communicate about your topic. Document these in single words, phrases, or sentences. Then, select the single most important point you truly want to make. No more!

From here, write three to seven points you want to share about that main point. Turn these points into sentences, and then expand them into paragraphs. You're now on your way to a first draft!

If I sound passionate about writing, it's because I am!

Before I began to trust myself as a writer, I came up against wall after wall after wall of resistance. I could have given up. But no wall was going to stop me from unleashing the true purpose I felt God had planned for me.

Almost everything worthwhile I'm doing today is a result of God helping me to overcome my own challenges, my own doubts, my own walls. And writing was no exception.

You have the power to scale your own walls, too. Trust me. No, *trust Him!*

Wrapping up: The worst thing I ever wrote

The worst thing I ever wrote was better than the best speech I ever gave.

I've actually given some decent speeches, but the things I've written always seem to resonate better with me, and with my audience. My point here is, I know what I'm good at. And what I'm not. And I know what I enjoy doing (writing), and what I don't so much enjoy (public speaking).

Know this about yourself as well. Write for your business if you enjoy it. Pursue speaking engagements if you enjoy that.

Either way, plunge in to what you truly love, and God will use it to bless others and will bless you along the way.

While you don't need to write or speak in order to have a successful indie consulting career, you *will* have greater success if you can write or speak and do it entertainingly.

For us indies, writing and speaking reside in the same category as marketing. We can't hide behind either at the beginning of our journey and expect our business to catch hold and grow. They can, however, propel our business to new heights once we've established a trusted network and client base on which they can ride. *That's a promise!*

Speaking of promises, that's the topic of our final chapter...!

CHAPTER 7

Questions for Guidance and Action

1. Do you plan to write as part of your business development? If yes, at what point in your business do you plan to start? What must you have accomplished before you begin to write? What media will you use and why?

2. Do you like to speak in public? Do you plan to use speaking as part of your business development strategy? If yes, at what point and what must you accomplish before you begin to seek out speaking engagements?

3. What is the single biggest action you will take today to move yourself closer to a client engagement?

4. What is the next single biggest action you will take?

5. And the next?

UNSELLING NOTES

_____

_____

_____

_____

_____

_____

_____

_____

_____

_____

_____

_____

_____

_____

_____

_____

_____

_____

_____

_____

_____

_____

_____

_____

_____

_____

_____

_____

_____

_____

_____

_____

_____

"Yes, but as you can see on page 57 of our agreement, having my fingers crossed does in fact constitute a legally binding excuse."

CHAPTER 8

Promises, Promises

A person who promises a gift but doesn't give it is
like clouds and wind that bring no rain.

Proverbs 25:14

~ Key Point ~

Delivering for clients means keeping the promises you've made, and this builds your integrity, and your business.

The red Lamborghini you can't drive

All this talk about networking, helping, educating, marketing, writing, and speaking is great, but without clients, this is no different than owning a shiny red Lamborghini without the ability to shift it into drive. It just sits in your driveway.

People can see it and enjoy looking at it. But you can't prove what it's capable of doing.

Until you engage a client, people can listen to you all day long, but there's no proof or believability that you can deliver on the most important thing: *Your promises.*

And that promise is simply that you can make the difference—make the impact—that you've been telling everyone you can make.

Deliver for clients, and you will prove that all of the promises you've been making in your networking, educating, marketing, writing, and speaking are real. And people want to be a part of something real.

A $40,000 lesson

Early in my CIO search business, before I had formalized anything (including contracts), I was introduced to a company needing to hire a CIO. I emailed back and forth with the company. Other search firms had not been successful for them, even after several months of effort.

I told my contact at the company that I wouldn't be able to take on the search, but I had someone in mind who might be a fit for them. I asked if I could present him. "Yes, please do," they responded.

I presented the candidate. They interviewed him, loved him, and hired him. I sent the invoice.

They didn't pay. Ever.

I emailed and called the company a few times. No response.

A sick feeling spilled into my gut, and then just hung there.

This company had no intention of paying. Yes, I should have gotten the agreement in place first, that was 100 percent my failure. The client knew that I had placed this individual with them but took advantage of me and the lack of agreement.

My mistake cost me about $40,000 of income.

These types of things happen. It's something that any business owner needs to expect. At the same time, we can protect ourselves. We can implement simple business processes (agreement first, service delivery second), and use solid agreements that equally protect the client and our business.

You can bet that I haven't made that mistake again. I also didn't wallow in this failure. That wouldn't have helped me in any way. I promised myself that I wouldn't send candidates to a client anymore without an agreement in place, and I doubly promised myself that I would always treat clients the way I would like to be treated.

I was certainly disappointed in myself. But, I would much rather be me and reside on this side of the equation than on the other side. I would rather keep my promises and the reputation that comes with it. I'm good with that.

Take care of your clients, and your clients will...

... do whatever they want to do.

What I mean is, clients are human just like we are, and we humans are mostly predictable. Mostly. We all have our moments of weakness, though. We'll not pay when we should, take the money when we shouldn't, take the credit for someone else's work, hide a mistake.

Each of these actions, and a multitude of others, chips away at who we are and the integrity on which we're trying to build our business. It also weakens our witness to others. After all, we're not just representing ourselves and our businesses, but also our God and Savior. So, while clients may be unpredictable at times, we need to be very predictable.

It doesn't matter what your clients do. Not one bit. What matters is what you and I do. How we, as sinners saved by grace, behave and treat others.

So in everything, do to others what you would have them do to you, for this sums up the Law and the Prophets.

Matthew 7:12

In business, your reputation will follow you, but it will also precede you. It can bring you business and opportunities, or cut them off.

Keep your promises. Deliver for your clients. Use solid agreements that equally protect both parties. Most of us would prefer a handshake to an agreement, but agreements are simply a necessary part of doing business. They exist to document the promises made to each other, setting clear expectations for engagement specifics like timeline, scope, deliverables, rates, fees, expenses, payments, and ownership of work, all with the intent of heading off disagreements.

No, not every client will take care of you, no matter how well you take care of them. Most will, but not all. Take care of them well, anyway. Even if they pay slower than promised, or not at all. Or if they cut engagements short. Or ask for more out of you than you agreed to deliver. You need to be prepared for these situations. Most of all, though, be prepared to always do the right thing—it's absolutely worth running your business with this mindset.

We are not of this world. Nor are we defined by our business, our income, our bank account balance, or even our successes or failures. We have a higher purpose.

> *You are the light of the world. A town built on a hill cannot be hidden. Neither do people light a lamp and put it under a bowl. Instead they put it on its stand, and it gives light to everyone in the house. In the same way, let your light shine before others, that they may see your good deeds and glorify your Father in heaven.*
>
> Matthew 5:14-16

Flywheelin' indie style

Let's shift gears. Imagine your indie business as a vehicle—your dream car. Maybe even that red Lamborghini. It can be old or new, classy or sporty, a souped-up muscle car or an exotic luxury sedan, on road or off.

Now imagine that dream car as the vehicle for your life—it's your life, your vision, your true purpose. It will be what takes you from zero to sixty, from a dusty dream to the deepest fulfillment for your life.

Now imagine your vehicle is ready for the road. Ready to engage clients—to take all the networking, helping, and educating you've been doing, and put the pedal to the metal.

But before we pop the clutch and drop the hammer on our souped-up new life, let's look under the hood.

Under the hood you'll find your indie engine. And inside your engine is a flywheel.

A flywheel is simply a mechanical wheel. It takes a lot of force to spin it around just one time—especially the first time. But, with each subsequent rotation, there's less resistance to forward motion.

The real magic of a flywheel? It stores up energy. This stored energy can be deployed later, when you most need it. As a flywheel picks up speed, it eventually takes on a life of its own by pulling in energy stored up from earlier efforts to spin it.

This flywheel metaphor is exactly what I experienced with my own business vehicle.

All of the networking, helping, educating, and client work I invested in built up, like the energy stored in a flywheel, and then paid off—incoming referrals trickled in early in my business, but took on a life of their own several years in. The continual effort and patience—as well as the promises I kept—eventually put me in the unselling life I'm now living.

You can make this happen for your business and life as well.

Until you have a client, though, the flywheel inside your engine isn't engaged. It just spins and spins, unable to do the job of storing energy and creating momentum for your business. You're stuck in park, foot pressed heavy on the gas.

Without clients, all of the networking, helping, and educating you've done up to this point simply revs the engine. It takes clients to engage the flywheel and put your vehicle into drive.

Engaging your first client is thrilling. It's the point you've been waiting for, when you get to prove yourself and bring your indie business (your indie flywheel) roaring to life.

Every client you engage turns your flywheel another full rotation. With each turn, you store more energy—credibility, believability, and trust. Referrals pick up, and soon, your business takes on a life of its own.

How to fully engage the unselling flywheel

In this unselling model, clients are more than just a source of income. They're also a relationship and a source of future business. With each client, you are:

- Solving strategic business problems, adding value, making a difference

- Expanding your network of people who know you, know what you can do, and trust you

- Creating experiences that you can include in your blogs, articles, speeches, and books

- Continually improving—learning and growing through successes, failures, and mistakes

- Building a reputation for delivering on your promises

The fruits of unselling

At least half of my incoming referrals are now through clients I've previously served, versus from my referral network. I love this balance of incoming work. If you serve clients with quality and integrity, and also continually grow and serve your referral network, you will experience this same ever-growing, robust balance of incoming business. Not only are the core roots of your business strong (a deep and broad referral network), but new and healthy roots (clients) will continually spring out as well.

This is the abundance that flows from a faith-filled, unselling approach to indie consulting and business development—no selling, cold-calling, or prospecting needed. Just faith, trust, and genuineness of heart.

Unselling forever

It has been over fourteen years since I began this journey to an unselling life. Through God's guiding hand, I overcame the temptations to give up along the way—all of those obstacles that littered my path and the frustrations that beat me down all too often. Fourteen years later I have an even stronger faith to lean on, knowing that as long as I continue to pursue God and His path for me, I can succeed in this unselling life, and continue to do more of what I love and was placed here to do.

And you can experience this too.

With each client you engage and successfully deliver for, you are turning your flywheel one more rotation. Each rotation stores energy—energy that will soon allow your business to take on a life of its own, with referrals showing up when you least expect them.

And more clients beget more clients. But only if you keep your indie engine humming through networking, helping, educating, and keeping your promises.

Believe God; don't just believe *in* Him. Trust His promises, and boldly live them out. We act boldly when we let go of our own limitations and trust God completely, as if there's no such thing as failure, no hurdles, no setbacks. Nothing is out to stop us from doing what we know God has put us here to do.

...being confident of this, that He who began a good work in you will carry it on to completion until the day of Christ Jesus.

Philippians 1:6

You are on the path to an unselling life—that point at which you get to say "No" to work you don't want, so that you can say "Yes" to the life you are truly after.

This is your path. No one else's. You are free in Christ to take this journey.

Along the way, pursue God and His Son wholeheartedly, make decisions based on *whose* you are, and be your genuine self.

Finally, each and every day on your journey...

Take delight in the LORD, and he will give you the desires of your heart.

Psalm 37:4

CHAPTER 8

Questions for Guidance and Action

1. What vehicle are you driving on your indie journey?

2. What promises will you be making to your clients?

3. Have you had your first successful client engagement? If yes, how are you planning to leverage that success to find more?

4. What three lessons did you learn that will make you better next time?

5. What is the single biggest action you will take today to move yourself closer to a client engagement?

6. What is the next single biggest action you will take?

7. And the next?

UNSELLING NOTES

Further Reading

See, I am doing a new thing! Now it springs up; do you not perceive it?
I am making a way in the wilderness and streams in the wasteland.

Isaiah 43:19

I'd like to share with you a few of the books and authors that have been important to me on my journey. I hope you find some new friends from among the list.

Christian Faith

The Blessed Life: Unlocking the Rewards of Generous Living – Robert Morris
Hand Me Another Brick – Charles R. Swindoll
The Journey of Desire – John Eldredege
Leadership Promises for Every Day – John C. Maxwell (I wore out this daily devotional!)
The Purpose Driven Life – Rick Warren

The Ragamuffin Gospel – Brennan Manning
Growing Strong in the Seasons of Life – Charles R. Swindoll
What's So Amazing About Grace? – Philip Yancey

Personal Growth

Braving the Wilderness – Brené Brown, PhD
Growing Up Again – Jean Illsley Clarke
The Highly Sensitive Person – Elaine Aron, PhD
How to Stop Worrying and Start Living – Dale Carnegie
How to Win Friends & Influence People – Dale Carnegie
I Thought It Was Just Me (but it isn't) – Brené Brown, PhD
The Introvert Advantage – Marti Olsen Laney, PsyD
Learned Optimism – Martin Seligman, PhD
Now, Discover Your Strengths – Marcus Buckingham and Donald O. Clifton
Quiet – Susan Cain
The 7 Habits of Highly Effective People – Stephen R. Covey
The Success Principles – Jack Canfield

Leadership

The Five Dysfunctions of a Team – Patrick Lencioni
Good to Great – Jim Collins
Primal Leadership – Daniel Goleman

Writing

Bird by Bird – Anne Lamott
On Writing – Stephen King
The War of Art – Steven Pressfield

Business

The E-Myth Revisited – Michael Gerber
The Goal – Eliyahu Goldratt
In Search of Excellence – Thomas J. Peters and Robert H. Waterman, Jr.
Purple Cow – Seth Godin
Selling the Invisible – Harry Beckwith
The Tipping Point – Malcolm Gladwell

90064720R00086

Made in the USA
San Bernardino, CA
14 October 2018